HIGH TRAIL COOKERY

HIGH TRAIL COOKERY

All-Natural, Home-Dried, Palate-Pleasing
Meals for the Backpacker

Linda Frederick Yaffe

Chicago Review Press

Printed in the United States of America by McNaughton &
  Gunn, Inc., Lithographers.
First Edition
Published by Chicago Review Press, 814 North Franklin
  Street, Chicago, IL 60610

Library of Congress Cataloging-in-Publication Data

Yaffe, Linda Frederick.
  High trail cookery: all-natural, home-dried, palate-pleasing
  meals for the backpacker / Linda Frederick Yaffe. — 1st ed.
        p.   cm.
  Includes index.
  ISBN 1-55652-056-5 : $9.95
  1. Outdoor cookery. 2. Backpacking. I. Title.
TX823.Y34   1989   89-30727
641.5'78—dc19   CIP

Cover design by Julie Smith.
Inside illustrations by the author.

This book is dedicated to pleasure in the
out-of-doors, with thanks to my partner,
Stuart Yaffe, and in memory of my mother,
Pearl Maps Frederick: 1906–1988.

Contents

CHAPTER ONE

Camp Cookery in Your Kitchen

Why Dry?

They've been hiking or biking since dawn. Now the sun is setting, and they're hungry. They're too tired to cook, but they'll soon be eating a delicious hot dinner. They pull from their pack a small pot and a packet of dried Shrimp Creole. A few minutes later, they are enjoying a homemade meal, spicy and satisfying.

High Trail Cookery makes this scenario possible. It was written to enable you to enjoy your next backpacking trip without lugging heavy fresh or canned ingredients in your pack, without the chore of cooking on the trail, and without squandering food dollars on tasteless, expensive commercially-dried foods. *High Trail Cookery* will show you how to cook, dry, and store complete all-natural meals at home, using a dehydrator, an oven, and sunlight. With it, you can prepare all your meals in advance, so that on the trail you can forget cooking, prop your feet on a rock, and enjoy the scenery.

Why dry? First, to enhance your camping pleasure. But there are other advantages, too.

Quality and Choice

Eating good-tasting, nutritious hot foods on the trail is one hundred percent practical with *High Trail Cookery*. Now you can create your own convenience foods and enjoy quality meals free of additives and preservatives no matter where you are. Choose the foods you enjoy, for good taste and health.

Economy

Home-dried foods are inexpensive to make, light in weight, and low in volume. A fine quality home dehydrator can be purchased for less than the cost of one week's supply of commercially-dried food for four people.

Simple Home Preparation

Choose your favorite meals from the backpack recipes in Chapter Two, Three, Four, and Five. Select top quality, fresh ingredients from your garden or the market. Cook a meal just as you would prepare tonight's dinner, then dehydrate the food in your oven or dehydrator. Save time by preparing extra servings; use some today, and dry the rest.

Less Fuel, Weight, and Equipment

Well-seasoned, hearty foods combined into one-pot meals are best for backpacking: soups, stews, and casseroles. All the backpack meals in this book use only one pot in the field. The foods are completely cooked at home; in camp, meals are simply brought to a boil, stirred, and served.

Food Drying Techniques

For thousands of years humans have dried foods to enhance their diets. Drying works via heat and air circulation, which remove most of the food's moisture and keep microorganisms from growing. For best results,

- Use quality ingredients: fresh herbs, fine cheese, fruit at its peak of ripeness.

- Chop or slice food uniformly for even drying.

- Dry strong-smelling foods, such as fish or onions, separately.

- Preheat oven or dehydrator for 10 minutes.

- Check food frequently as it dries; turn and shift it several times.

- Drying times vary. To preserve perishable foods for long-term storage (up to one year), dry them thoroughly. Drying times listed in this book are for a standard commercial dehydrator equipped with electrical heat source and fan.

Drying Foods Using a Dehydrator

Dehydrators are the most convenient method of drying and yield the best quality product. Food can be dried at any time of year, in any weather, without interfering with kitchen activities.

Commercial dehydrators can be purchased by mail from Sears Roebuck and Co. (nationwide outlets), Campmor, P.O. Box 997-F, Paramus, NJ 07653-0997, and Recreational Equipment Inc., P.O. Box 88125, Seattle, WA 98138-0125. To build your own dehydrator, contact your United States Department of

Agriculture Extension for information and dehydrator plans.

To dry solid foods, such as sliced vegetables, fruits, and jerky, place food directly on drying trays. Turn the food once while drying.

To dry liquid foods, such as soup or stew, use plastic wrap. Place pieces of plastic wrap over the middle of drying trays, leaving 1½ inches to 2 inches of space between edge of wrap and edge of tray, allowing air to circulate. Masking tape can be used, if needed, to hold wrap in place.

Spread a thin layer of food on the plastic wrap. As the food dries, turn and shift it, breaking up large pieces. Check the food, and shift it, every 1 to 3 hours.

Drying Foods Using an Oven

All meals in *High Trail Cookery* can be dried in your oven.

To prepare your electric oven for drying, remove the top heating element. If this element is not removable, place an empty baking sheet on the oven's top shelf, and dry food on the lower shelves.

Turn the oven to its lowest setting, 140–150°F. Place an oven thermometer next to the drying food to keep the temperature within this range. Leave the oven door partially open to allow air to circulate: 1 inch to 2 inches for an electric oven, 5 inches to 6 inches for a gas oven. An electric fan placed just outside the oven door, blowing air over the food, will greatly improve circulation.

To dry solid foods, such as sliced vegetables, fruits, and jerky, place food on several layers of fine mesh nylon net or nylon organdy, available at fabric shops. Set the nylon material on your oven racks.

To dry liquid foods, such as soups, spread them in a thin layer on oiled baking sheets.

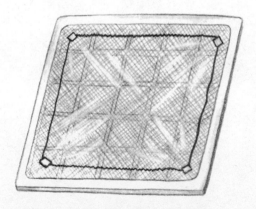

Drying tray covered with plastic wrap.

Oven-dried foods must be checked and shifted frequently to prevent scorching, particularly during the last one-third of drying time. To reduce heat, open the oven door a few more inches.

Drying food using an oven.

Drying Foods Using the Sun

Nonperishable foods—uncooked fruits and vegetables—can be sun dried. See Index for Dried Fruit and Vegetable Chips. Perishable foods, such as meat or cooked beans, must be dried in your oven or dehydrator.

Sun drying works best in areas with consistent hot sun and low humidity, where the air is free of excessive dust and pollution.

Baking sheets make simple drying trays. Window screens are good trays, providing better air circulation; cover the screens with cheesecloth so food does not touch the galvanized metal.

Lay the sliced fruits or vegetables on drying trays, and cover the food with cheesecloth. Turn the slices once or twice a day. Bring the trays indoors at sundown; replace them outdoors in the morning.

Fruits and vegetables can be sun dried in one to four days.

Keeping Dried Food

Dried foods must be kept cool and dry, and protected from exposure to air and light.

Packaging

Before packing dried food, let it stand at room temperature on the drying trays for several hours, or overnight. The food will cool, continue to dry, and "condition." This cooling period will prevent mold from forming.

When the dried food is completely cool, place it in small, sturdy plastic bags. Place one or more servings of food in a single bag, according to your camping or traveling plans. Press the bags firmly before sealing, expelling as much air as possible. Put each bag inside a second plastic bag.

Store the bags of food inside a metal container with a tight-fitting lid. If a metal container isn't available, store the individual servings in a black plastic bag. When you are ready to camp or travel, the individually-bagged servings can go directly into your knapsack.

Dried food can also be stored in clean, dry screw-top glass or ceramic containers. They should be dark-colored. Bag the containers in plastic for an extra layer of protection.

Labeling

Dried foods look alike; label each batch of food as you package it. Using ordinary paper, cut very small labels, 2½ inches by 1 inch. Record the name of the meal, the date food was dried, number of servings, and instructions for preparing the food in the field.

New Eng. Clam Chowder   4 Servings
Cover w/water; boil, stir, serve.   2-18-89

Insert the label between the two plastic bags, so the ink isn't touching the food. Seal the outside bag tightly, expelling as much air as possible.

All dried meals in this book are simply prepared in the field by covering them with water, boiling, stirring, and serving. Instructions may seem unnecessary, but be sure to include them so any member of your party can prepare any food.

Storing

Most dried foods will keep for one year, some even longer.

Nonperishable foods, such as fruits or vegetables, can be stored in a cool, dark, dry area, such as a closet in the coolest, driest room in your house. The kitchen is too warm; the basement is too damp. Perishable foods, such as those containing meats or cooked beans, are best stored in the refrigerator for up to one year, or in the freezer for even longer. If you live in a cold climate and have a cool, dry room in your house, you can safely store your more perishable dried foods there. If you live in a warm climate, the refrigerator is a better choice.

Fish or beef jerky can be stored in your refrigerator for six months, then carried in your knapsack for two weeks without refrigeration.

Field Equipment

High Trail Cookery's one-pot method requires very few pieces of field equipment.

Aluminum Pot

Carry only one pot; leave your frying pan and extra pots at home. Choose the lightest weight aluminum pot you can find. Flea markets and thrift shops are good sources for pots and silverware. One person needs a one-quart pot; two or three people need a two-quart pot; four people need a three-quart pot. To save weight, you may leave the pot lid at home and substitute a piece of heavy-duty aluminum foil.

Store your pot in a heavy plastic bag.

Aluminum pot and lid.

Cups

Carry one cup per person. No plates or bowls are needed. Stainless steel Sierra cups are durable and versatile; filled to the brim, they hold exactly one cup. Lexan plastic cups are another durable choice.

Sierra cup.

Teaspoons

Carry one lightweight stainless steel teaspoon per person. No forks or table knives are needed. One member of the party needs to carry a sharp folding knife, to share.

Stove and Fuel Container

Choose a lightweight backpack stove that burns butane, propane, kerosene, or white gasoline.

Windscreen

This lightweight aluminum screen greatly improves the efficiency of your stove or small campfire. Cut two pieces of heavy-duty aluminum foil, each 28 inches long and 18 inches wide. Put the two pieces together, shiny side out. Fold down 2 inches from the top, and 2 inches up from the bottom.

To store, fold into quarters and keep with your cooking pot. In camp, open the screen and crimp the foil to curve around your stove or fire. Secure the folded bottom of screen with small, heavy rocks.

Aluminum windscreen.

Nylon Net, Sponge, and Soap

An 8-inch square of regular mesh nylon net makes an effective, almost weightless, scrubber. After cleanup, remove water and food particles by briskly shaking the net. Nylon net is available at any fabric shop. A small household sponge wipes moisture from wet equipment. Small bottles of biodegradable liquid soap can be purchased at camping supply shops.

Plastic Food Tubes

Nut butters, jelly, honey, mustard, margarine, and baby food can be carried in refillable plastic tubes, available at camping supply shops.

Using the Recipes

Before you begin to cook, read the entire recipe. The following healthful ingredients work well in these recipes:

- Instant nonfat dry milk instead of whole milk.

- Table spread containing a large percentage of vegetable oil, instead of regular margarine or butter.

- Soy cheese, available in Cheddar or mozzarella types, instead of dairy cheese, in any recipe requiring cooked or melted cheese.

- Frozen cholesterol-free egg product, or egg whites, instead of whole eggs.

Plastic food tube.

Nylon net, sponge, and liquid soap.

CHAPTER TWO
Backpack Breakfasts and Brunches

Vegetable Kugel

1. Preheat oven to 350°F.
2. Grate, then drain in a colander:

5	**small new potatoes, scrubbed but not peeled**
1	**onion**
2	**medium carrots, scrubbed but not peeled**
2	**cloves garlic.**

3. Tightly wrap the grated vegetables in a cloth towel, then squeeze out as much moisture as possible.
4. Beat together in a large bowl:

1	**whole egg plus 2 egg whites**
2	**cups (16 ounces) plain lowfat yogurt**
½	**cup dry milk**
¼	**cup matzoh meal or whole wheat flour**
¼	**cup olive oil**
¼	**cup water**
2	**tablespoons honey**
1	**teaspoon sea salt**
1	**teaspoon fresh thyme, or**
½	**teaspoon dried.**

5. Add the grated vegetables, along with:

10	**sprigs parsley, minced**
¼	**pound cheese, grated.**

6. Stir together, then spread in a 9″ x 13″ oiled glass casserole dish. Bake at 350°F for 40 minutes, or until toothpick inserted in center comes out clean.
7. Spread on plastic-covered trays and dehydrate for 5 hours at 145°F.
8. To rehydrate, cover with water, boil, stir, and serve.

Sweet Potatoes and Scrambled Eggs

1. Preheat oven to 425°F.
2. Scrub but do not peel:

    4   medium sweet potatoes or yams.

    Slice off the ends. Place the potatoes on a baking sheet and bake for 35 minutes.
3. Cool the potatoes slightly, then dice them.
4. Heat a large cast-iron skillet over high heat. Add:

    1   tablespoon corn oil.

    When the oil is hot, add:

    1   onion, finely chopped.

    Cook and stir the onion for 3 minutes, then add the diced potatoes. Reduce heat to medium-low and cook for 5 minutes.
5. Beat together:

    2   whole eggs plus 3 egg whites
    1   tablespoon water
    ¼   teaspoon sea salt
    ¼   teaspoon freshly ground black pepper.

    Pour the egg mixture over the potatoes. Cook, stirring gently, until the eggs are set. Pour over the eggs:

    1   tablespoon fresh lemon juice.
6. Spread on plastic-covered trays and dehydrate for 5 hours at 145°F.
7. To rehydrate, cover with water, boil, stir, and serve.

Vegetable Scrambled Eggs or Tofu

1. Prepare:

   **4   servings Stir-Fried Vegetables
   (see Chapter Seven).**

2. Break into a bowl:

   **2   whole eggs plus 4 egg whites,
   beaten with 2 tablespoons water
   or**

   **1   pound firm tofu, rinsed and
   drained, crumbled, mixed with
   hot sauce to taste and ¼
   teaspoon ground tumeric.**

3. When the vegetables are cooked, push them to the sides of the pot. Pour into the center of the pot:

   1   teaspoon corn or soy oil.

   When the oil is hot, add the eggs or tofu. Stir for a few minutes, then mix them with the vegetables.

4. Correct seasoning if necessary. Add:

   2   cups grated cheese.

   Stir gently just until cheese melts.

5. Spread the mixture on plastic-covered trays and dehydrate for 5½ hours at 145°F.

6. To rehydrate, cover with water, boil, stir, and serve.

Tofu Omelette

1. Heat in an omelette pan over high heat:

   2   tablespoons olive oil.

   When the oil is hot, add:

   8   whole fresh mushrooms, finely chopped.

   Sauté for 3 minutes, or until browned.

2. Beat together in a bowl:

   2   whole eggs plus 2 egg whites
   2   green onions, minced
   1   pound firm tofu, rinsed, drained, and finely chopped
   2   tablespoons tamari soy sauce
   1   tablespoon water
   Dash of cayenne pepper.

3. Pour the egg mixture over the mushrooms. Reduce heat. Lift the mixture to allow uncooked portion to flow underneath.

4. Fold omelette in half. Cover and cook over very low heat for 1 minute.

5. Spread the omelette on plastic-covered trays and dehydrate for 4½ hours at 145°F.

6. To rehydrate, barely cover with water, boil, stir, and serve.

Spanish Omelette

1. Prepare:

   > **Thick Tomato Sauce (see Chapter Seven) or use 2 cups commercial sauce.**

   Simmer the sauce in a cast-iron skillet. Add:

   > **3   jalapeño chilies, fresh or canned, minced.**

2. Cook:

   > **4   servings Millet or Bulgur Wheat (see Chapter Seven).**

3. Prepare:

   > **2   plain Three-Egg Omelettes (see Index).**

4. Blend together the cooked grain, tomato sauce, and omelettes.

5. Spread on plastic-covered trays and dehydrate for 5 hours at 145°F.

6. To rehydrate, cover with water, boil, stir, and serve.

Vegetable and Sausage Frittata

1. Preheat oven to 350°F.
2. Heat a cast-iron Dutch oven over high heat. Add:

   2 tablespoons olive oil.

3. When the oil is hot, add:

   3½ cups grated or finely minced vegetables, such as yellow onion, potato, zucchini, broccoli, eggplant, bell pepper.

   Reduce heat when necessary, and sauté the vegetables until light brown.

4. Add:

   5 small sausages, cut into ¼-inch crosswise slices—choose Italian meat sausage, or TVP (vegetable) sausage, available in frozen food section of market.

5. When vegetables and sausages are well browned, turn off heat and add:

   1 cup fresh bean sprouts

   1 clove garlic, minced
   1 whole tomato, minced
   1 tablespoon dried Italian seasoning
   ⅛ teaspoon cayenne pepper.

6. When the mixture has cooled, add and stir thoroughly:

   6 ounces any well-flavored cheese, grated
   2 ounces Parmesan cheese, grated
   2 whole eggs plus 2 egg whites, beaten.

7. Spread the mixture evenly in a 9″ x 13″ oiled glass casserole dish.
8. Bake at 350°F for 25–30 minutes, or until golden brown.
9. Spread the frittata on plastic-covered trays and dehydrate for 5 hours at 145°F.
10. To rehydrate, barely cover with water, boil, stir, and serve.

Cottage Cheese Casserole

1. Preheat oven to 350°F.
2. Steam for 5 minutes, or until just tender:

   1½ **cups broccoli flowerettes, chopped.**

3. Beat together:

   1 **whole egg plus 2 egg whites**
   1 **cup (8 ounces) lowfat cottage cheese**
   ¾ **cup whole wheat bread crumbs**
   1 **small onion, minced**
   ¼ **cup fresh lemon juice**
   2 **teaspoons minced fresh basil, or 1 teaspoon dried**
   ¼ **teaspoon sea salt**
   ¼ **teaspoon freshly ground black pepper.**

4. Add the steamed broccoli to the egg mixture.
5. Pour into a shallow, oiled glass casserole dish.
6. Bake at 350°F for 25 minutes, or until toothpick inserted in center comes out clean.
7. Spread the casserole on plastic-covered trays and dehydrate for 4½ hours at 145°F.
8. To rehydrate, cover with water, boil, stir, and serve.

Baked Pasta with Eggs and Cheddar

1. Prepare:

4	servings Fresh Pasta (see Chapter Seven) or use 12 ounces any dried commercial pasta.

   Cook the pasta until it is barely tender, then drain it in a colander.

2. Preheat oven to 350°F.

3. Oil a 9″ x 14″ glass casserole dish.

4. Spread the cooked pasta in the dish, and sprinkle it with:

8	ounces very sharp Cheddar cheese, grated
2	ounces Parmesan cheese, grated
1	bell pepper, minced
2	jalapeño chilies, fresh or canned, minced
2	cloves garlic, minced
2	tablespoons fresh rosemary, minced, or 2 teaspoons dried.

5. Beat together in a small bowl:

1	whole egg plus 2 egg whites
2¼	cups milk
½	teaspoon sea salt
⅛	teaspoon ground cinnamon
	Dash of Worcestershire sauce.

   Pour the egg mixture over the pasta.

6. Bake the casserole for 35 minutes, or until browned.

7. Spread on plastic-covered trays and dehydrate for 5 hours at 145°F.

8. To rehydrate, barely cover with water, boil, stir, and serve.

Toiyabe Quiche

1. Preheat oven to 350°F.

2. Sauté over medium heat in a cast-iron skillet, until very lightly browned:

1	tablespoon olive oil
1	large onion, minced
1½	cups whole fresh mushrooms, minced.

3. Beat together in a large bowl:

2	whole eggs plus 2 egg whites
½	cup margarine, melted
1	small zucchini or other summer squash, grated
10	sprigs parsley, minced
½	pound Monterey Jack cheese, grated
1	cup (8 ounces) lowfat cottage cheese.

4. Mix together in a medium bowl:

½	cup whole wheat flour
1	teaspoon baking powder
1	teaspoon sea salt

   Dash of cayenne pepper.

5. Oil a 9" x 13" glass casserole dish.

6. Add the sautéed mushrooms and the flour mixture to the egg mixture. Blend thoroughly, then spread in the prepared dish.

7. Bake at 350°F for 35 minutes, or until toothpick inserted in center comes out clean.

8. Spread the quiche on plastic-covered trays and dehydrate for 5 hours at 145°F.

9. To rehydrate, barely cover with water, boil, stir, and serve.

Hominy Grits Soufflé

1. Preheat oven to 350°F.
2. Bring to a boil:

   6   cups water.
3. Gradually stir in:

   1½   cups quick-cooking grits.

   Reduce heat and cook the grits for 4 minutes, stirring occasionally.
4. Remove from heat and beat in, one at a time:

   2   whole eggs plus 2 egg whites.

   Add:

   8   ounces cheese, grated
   5   green onions, minced
   10   sprigs parsley, minced
   1   teaspoon honey
   1   teaspoon sea salt
   Hot sauce to taste
   6   strips bacon, cooked and crumbled (optional)
   ½   pound tofu, crumbled (optional).

   Beat thoroughly.
5. Spread the grits in a shallow, oiled glass casserole dish.
6. Bake at 350°F for 40–45 minutes, or until toothpick inserted in center comes out clean.
7. Spread on plastic-covered trays and dehydrate for 5 hours at 145°F.
8. To rehydrate, cover with water, boil, stir, and serve.

Breakfast Beans

Frijoles Refritos for breakfast.

1. Cook:

    **1½ cups dried pinto beans (see
    To Cook Dried Beans, Chapter
    Seven) or use 3¾ cups canned
    beans.**

    Drain the beans in a colander, reserving liquid.

2. Heat a cast-iron Dutch oven over high heat. Add:

    2 tablespoons soy or corn oil.

    When the oil is hot, add:

    1 large onion, minced.

    Sauté the onion, stirring constantly, for 2 minutes,
    then add half of the drained, cooked beans, ½ cup
    of the bean liquid, and:

    3 whole ripe tomatoes, chopped.

    Using a potato masher or the back of a large
    spoon, mash the beans.

3. Add the rest of the cooked beans to the pot, along
   with:

    **5 jalapeño chilies, fresh or canned,
    minced**

    1 clove garlic, minced

    1 tablespoon chili powder

    1 teaspoon cumin seed, crushed

    ½ teaspoon sea salt.

    Simmer the beans for 50 minutes, stirring
    occasionally and adding very small amounts of
    liquid if necessary; keep the mixture thick.

4. Turn off heat and add:

    1½ cups grated cheese

    5 green onions, minced.

5. Spread on plastic-covered trays and dehydrate for
   4½ hours at 145°F.

6. To rehydrate, barely cover with water, boil, stir,
   and serve.

7. Serve with:

    **Corn Tortillas or Gloria's Flour
    Tortillas (see Chapter Seven) or
    commercial tortillas.**

Potatoes and Beans

1. Cook:

   ⅝ cup dried pinto beans (see To Cook Dried Beans, Chapter Seven) or use 1¼ cups canned beans.

   Drain the beans in a colander; reserve the bean liquid.

2. Cover with water and simmer for 15 minutes, or until just tender:

   8 medium-sized new potatoes, scrubbed but not peeled.

   Drain the potatoes and dice them.

3. Heat in a cast-iron Dutch oven over high heat:

   2 tablespoons olive oil.

   When oil is hot, add:

   1 onion, minced.

   Stir-fry for 2 minutes, then add the diced potatoes. Cook, stirring occasionally, until the potatoes are browned.

4. Add the cooked beans to the potatoes, along with:

   ½ cup bean liquid
   4 whole ripe tomatoes, finely chopped
   2 cloves garlic, minced
   ½ teaspoon sea salt
   Hot sauce to taste.

   Simmer for 5 minutes. Correct seasoning if necessary.

5. Spread on plastic-covered trays and dehydrate for 5 hours at 145°F.

6. To rehydrate, cover with water, boil, stir, and serve.

Breakfast Tacos

1. Prepare:

    4   servings Stir-Fried Vegetables (see Chapter Seven).

2. Add to the vegetables and sauté:

    10   small sausages, cut into ¼-inch crosswise slices—choose any meat sausage, or TVP (vegetable) sausage, available in frozen food section of market.

3. When the vegetables and sausages are browned, add:

    3   whole ripe tomatoes, finely chopped

    2   tablespoons fresh minced oregano, or 1 tablespoon dried.

    Simmer for 5 minutes.

4. Spread on plastic-covered trays and dehydrate for 5½ hours at 145°F.

5. To rehydrate, barely cover with water, boil, stir, and serve.

6. Serve with:

    Gloria's Flour Tortillas (see Chapter Seven) or commercial flour tortillas.

Mild Breakfast Curry

1. Boil gently for 8 minutes, then cool:

    2 eggs.

    Shell, then chop the eggs finely. Set aside.

2. Heat in a cast-iron Dutch oven over high heat:

    2 tablespoons olive oil.

    When the oil is hot, add:

    1 large onion, minced.

    Stir-fry the onion until transparent, then add:

    4 small new potatoes, scrubbed but not peeled, minced.

3. Brown the vegetables, reducing heat to medium when necessary. Add:

    2 cups whole fresh mushrooms, finely chopped

    1 stalk broccoli, finely chopped.

    Cook, stirring occasionally, for 10 minutes.

4. Reduce heat to low and add:

    2 tablespoons whole wheat flour.

    Stir until the flour is toasted, then add very gradually:

    1½ cups bean liquid, stock, or milk.

5. Stir constantly until the sauce is thick and smooth, then add:

    1 teaspoon curry powder

    ½ teaspoon ground ginger

    ¼ teaspoon sea salt

    Cayenne pepper to taste.

6. Add the chopped hard-boiled eggs, along with:

    1 pound tofu, rinsed, drained, and crumbled.

7. Simmer gently for 5 minutes.

8. Cook:

    4 servings Couscous (see Chapter Seven).

9. Combine couscous and curry mixture.

10. Spread on plastic-covered trays and dehydrate for 5 hours at 145°F.

11. To rehydrate, cover with water, let stand briefly, boil, stir, and serve.

Hashed Brown Vegetables with Sausage

1. Grate and drain in a colander:

   **6   small new potatoes, scrubbed
   but not peeled**
   1   small eggplant
   2   small zucchini
   2   medium onions.

   Turn the grated vegetables out onto a cloth towel. Wrap the ends of the towel tightly and squeeze out as much moisture as possible.

2. Heat a cast-iron Dutch oven over high heat. Add:

   3   tablespoons olive oil.

   When the oil is hot, add the grated vegetables, along with:

   **2   cups whole fresh mushrooms,
   finely chopped**
   **10   small sausages, cut into ¼-inch
   crosswise slices—choose any
   meat sausage, or TVP (vegetable)
   sausage, available in frozen food
   section of market.**

3. Cook over high heat for 10 minutes, then reduce heat to medium and cook, stirring occasionally, for 20 minutes longer, or until vegetables are well browned.

4. Stir in:

   **½   cup freshly grated Parmesan
   cheese**
   2   cloves garlic, minced
   Sea salt to taste
   Hot sauce to taste.

5. Spread on plastic-covered trays and dehydrate for 5 hours at 145°F.

6. To rehydrate, barely cover with water, boil, stir, and serve.

Powerhouse Potatoes

A satisfying meal.

1. Bring to a boil in a large saucepan:

   1½ quarts water.

2. Add:

   6 medium-sized new potatoes, scrubbed but not peeled.

   Bring to a boil, then simmer the potatoes for 4 minutes. Drain them in a colander; let them cool.

3. Grate the potatoes.

4. Heat in a cast-iron Dutch oven:

   3 tablespoons olive oil.

   When the oil is hot, add:

   1 large onion, minced.

   Stir-fry the onion for 1 minute, then add the grated potatoes and cook, stirring occasionally, for 5 minutes. Reduce heat to medium-low and cook 5 minutes longer, or until vegetables are browned.

5. Reduce heat to low and add:

   1 whole ripe tomato, minced

   2 minced jalapeño peppers, fresh or canned, or cayenne pepper to taste

   ¾ teaspoon sea salt

   ½ teaspoon freshly ground black pepper.

   Cook for 3 minutes. Add:

   3 ounces sharp Cheddar cheese, grated

   8 ounces light cream cheese.

   Stir until cheese melts.

6. Turn off heat. Add:

   1 cup (8 ounces) plain yogurt.

7. Stir. Correct seasoning if necessary.

8. Spread the potatoes on plastic-covered trays and dehydrate for 6 hours at 145°F.

9. To rehydrate, cover with water, boil, stir, and serve.

Donburi

Japanese one-dish meal.

1. Cook:

   4   **servings Brown Rice (see Chapter Seven).**

2. Heat in a cast-iron Dutch oven over high heat:

   3   **tablespoons olive oil.**

   When the oil is hot, add:

   2   **medium zucchini, finely chopped.**

   Stir-fry for 1 minute, then add:

   1   **small eggplant, finely chopped.**

   Fry until browned, then add:

   1¼   **cups whole fresh mushrooms, chopped.**

   Reduce heat to medium and cook, stirring occasionally, for 5 minutes.

3. Beat together in a medium bowl:

   2   **whole eggs plus 2 egg whites**
   1   **pound firm tofu, rinsed and drained**
   1   **small bell pepper, finely chopped**
   5   **tablespoons tamari soy sauce**
   3   **tablespoons sherry**
   Cayenne pepper to taste.

4. Make a well in the center of the vegetables in the Dutch oven and pour in the egg mixture. Cook, stirring gently, until eggs are set.

5. Turn off heat and stir in:

   3   **green onions, minced.**

6. Blend together the rice and the vegetable-egg mixture. Spread on plastic-covered trays and dehydrate for 5½ hours at 145°F.

7. To rehydrate, cover with water, let stand briefly, boil, stir, and serve.

Creole Beans and Rice

1. Cook:

   1 cup dried pinto beans (see To Cook Dried Beans, Chapter Seven) or use 2¾ cups canned beans.

2. Drain the cooked beans, reserving the liquid.

3. Heat a cast-iron Dutch oven over high heat. Add:

   2 tablespoons olive oil.

   When the oil is hot, add:

   1 large onion, minced.

   Sauté the onion until it is evenly browned.

4. Reduce heat to low and add:

   6 whole ripe tomatoes, finely chopped

   1 large or 2 small bell peppers, finely chopped

   5 jalapeño peppers, fresh or canned, minced

   2 cloves garlic, minced

   2 teaspoons fresh minced thyme, or 1 teaspoon dried.

5. Add the cooked beans, along with:

   ½ cup reserved bean liquid

   ¼ cup Burgundy.

6. Partially cover and let simmer for 90 minutes.

7. Cook:

   4 servings Brown Rice (see Chapter Seven).

8. Add the cooked rice to the bean mixture, along with:

   1½ teaspoons sea salt
   Freshly ground black pepper to taste.

9. Spread on plastic-covered trays and dehydrate for 5 hours at 145°F.

10. To rehydrate, cover with water, let stand briefly, boil, stir, and serve.

Pan-Fried Noodles

1. Prepare:

   4   Servings Fresh Pasta (see Chapter Seven) or use 12 ounces dried commercial noodles.

   Cook the pasta until barely tender, then drain it in a colander.

2. Prepare:

   4   servings Stir-Fried Vegetables (see Chapter Seven).

   When the vegetables are partially cooked, reduce heat to medium and add the drained, cooked pasta. Cook, stirring occasionally, until vegetables and noodles are well browned, about 20 minutes.

3. Add:

   1   can water chestnuts, drained and minced.

   Stir and simmer for 3 minutes.

4. Turn off heat and add:

   1   cup raw bean sprouts.

5. Stir thoroughly. Spread on plastic-covered trays and dehydrate for 4½ hours at 145°F.

6. To rehydrate, barely cover with water, boil, stir, and serve.

High-Protein Granola

1. Brown in a cast-iron Dutch oven, stirring frequently, until golden:
   - ½ **cup whole wheat flour**
   - ½ **cup soya flour**
   - ½ **cup sesame seed**
   - ½ **cup wheat germ**
   - ½ **cup oat or wheat bran.**

2. Preheat oven to 300°F.

3. Heat gently in a small saucepan:
   - ½ **cup honey**
   - ½ **cup corn or soy oil.**

4. Add honey-oil mixture to flour mixture, along with:
   - ½ **teaspoon vanilla extract**
   - 1 **cup any unsalted nutmeats, chopped, or more to taste (try a combination of several nuts)**
   - ¾ **cup unsweetened shredded coconut**
   - 6 **cups rolled oats.**

5. Mix the granola thoroughly and spread it in a 9″ x 13″ glass casserole dish.

6. Pour evenly over the granola:
   - ½ **cup any fruit juice.**

7. Bake at 300°F for 30–35 minutes, stirring once during baking.

8. Cool completely, then double-bag and store in freezer until ready to use.

Granola Variations

Ten and a half cups

1. Prepare:

    High Protein Granola (see preceding recipe).

2. When granola has cooled to room temperature, add and blend in any of the following dried fruits. Use commercial or home-dried fruit (see Index).

    2   cups raisins or currants

    2   cups dried blueberries

    2   teaspoons ground cinnamon,
    1 teaspoon ground nutmeg, and
    2 cups dried apple slices, chopped

    2   cups dried dates, pitted and chopped

    1   teaspoon ground allspice, and
    2 cups dried banana chips, chopped

    1   teaspoon ground cinnamon,
    ⅛ teaspoon ground ginger, and
    2 cups dried peach slices, chopped.

Granola to Go

1. To package individual servings of granola for camping, place in individual 6½-inch square plastic sandwich bags:

    ⅝   cup **High Protein Granola (see preceding recipe)**

    ¼   cup **Milkman brand lowfat dry milk.**

2. Flatten the bag to exclude as much air as possible. Seal the bag tightly.

3. Shake the bag, mixing the granola and milk thoroughly.

4. To serve, pour ¼–½ cup fresh water into your cup. Add granola, a little at a time. Stir and enjoy.

Instant Highland Porridge

Unlike the commercial product, this oatmeal is delicious.

1. Stir together in the top half of a double boiler:

4	cups water
1¾	cups rolled oats
½	cup dry milk
¼	cup oat bran
¼	cup honey
1	tablespoon margarine
½	teaspoon ground cinnamon
½	teaspoon ground allspice
¼	teaspoon sea salt.

   Bring to a boil.

2. Place the pot over several inches of water in the bottom half of the double boiler, and simmer the porridge for at least 1 hour, stirring occasionally. If your wood stove is hot, put plenty of water in the double boiler and cook the porridge overnight in a cool spot on the wood stove.

3. Spread the porridge on plastic-covered trays and dehydrate for 4 hours at 145°F.

4. To rehydrate, cover with water, boil, stir, and serve.

5. To serve, mix some fresh water and instant dry milk in your cup or bowl. Add the heated porridge.

Crust for Pasties

1. Sift together in a medium bowl:

   1   cup whole wheat flour
   ¾   cup unbleached white flour
   ½   teaspoon baking powder.

   Resift the flour mixture.
2. Cut in:

   ½   cup (1 stick) margarine.
3. Add:

   4   tablespoons plus 1 teaspoon
        icewater.

   Gently blend with a fork, handling as little as possible. Form the dough into a ball.
4. Double-bag the dough, expelling as much air as possible. Chill the dough in the refrigerator for 12–24 hours.
5. Remove the dough from the refrigerator 2 hours before rolling, filling, and baking it.

Filling, folding, and crimping pasties.

35

Taboose Pass Cheese and Onion Pasties

1. Prepare:
   ### Crust for Pasties (see preceding recipe).
   Chill the dough overnight, and remove it from the refrigerator 2 hours before rolling and baking it.

2. Heat a cast-iron skillet over high heat. Add:
   1   tablespoon olive oil.
   When the oil is hot, add:
   2   yellow onions, chopped.
   Quickly stir-fry the onions until browned, about 2 minutes. Turn off heat and set aside.

3. Preheat oven to 450°F.

4. Grate into a bowl:
   1¼   pounds any cheese.
   Add the fried onions, along with:
   3   jalapeño chilies, fresh or canned, minced.
   Stir the mixture and set aside.

5. Divide the pastie dough into 12 pieces. On a lightly floured board, roll out each piece into a circle, handling the dough as little as possible. Spread the 12 circles on a lightly floured board or countertop.

6. Spoon the cheese mixture onto the dough circles. Fold them in half. Seal and crimp the edges tightly.

7. Place the pasties on an ungreased baking sheet. Prick the tops of the pasties several times with a fork.

8. Bake at 450°F for 15 minutes, then reduce heat to 325°F and bake for 15 minutes longer.

9. Cook completely, then wrap pasties individually in plastic wrap. Double-bag them in plastic.

Apple-Cheese Pasties

1. Prepare:

   Crust for Pasties (see preceding recipe).

   Chill the dough overnight, and remove it from the refrigerator 2 hours before rolling and baking it.

2. Mix together in a large bowl:

   Juice of 1 fresh lemon
   6 tart apples, peeled, cored, and sliced very thin
   ⅓ cup honey
   2 tablespoons whole wheat flour
   1 tablespoon apple juice
   1 tablespoon cornstarch
   2 teaspoons ground cinnamon
   1 teaspoon ground allspice
   1 teaspoon vanilla extract
   ½ teaspoon grated nutmeg.

   Let the mixture stand at room temperature for 60 minutes.

3. Preheat oven to 450°F.

4. Grate:

   ¼ pound sharp Cheddar cheese.

   Add the grated cheese to the apple mixture. Stir.

5. Divide the pastie dough into 12 pieces. On a lightly floured board, roll out each piece into a circle, handling the dough as little as possible. Spread the 12 circles on a lightly floured board or countertop.

6. Spoon the apple filling onto the dough circles. Fold the pasties in half. Seal and crimp the edges tightly.

7. Place the pasties on an ungreased baking sheet. Prick the tops of the pasties several times with a fork.

8. Bake the pasties at 450°F for 15 minutes, then reduce heat to 325°F and bake for 15 minutes longer.

9. Cool completely, then wrap pasties individually in plastic wrap. Double-bag them in plastic.

Blueberry Muffins

1. Preheat oven to 400°F.
2. Line muffin tins with:
   Paper baking cups.
3. Mix together in a large bowl:

1	**cup whole wheat flour**
1	**cup unbleached white flour**
3	**teaspoons baking powder**
1	**tablespoon wheat germ.**

4. Beat together in a separate bowl:

¾	**cup water**
¼	**cup dry milk**
½	**cup honey**
⅓	**cup soy or corn oil**
1	**whole egg plus 1 egg white.**

5. Wash and drain in a colander:

1	**cup fresh blueberries (frozen or canned may be used).**

6. Pour the liquid ingredients into the dry ones, and stir very briefly. Do not beat. Gently stir in the drained blueberries. Spoon the dough into the baking cups.
7. Bake at 400°F for 18–20 minutes, or until light brown.

Spicy Apple Muffins

These muffins pack well and stay fresh for many days.

1. Preheat oven to 375°F.
2. Line muffin tins with:

   Paper baking cups.
3. Beat together in a large bowl:

1¼	**cups water**
¼	**cup dry milk**
½	**cup brown sugar**
½	**cup soy or corn oil**
1	**egg.**
4. Mix together in a medium bowl:

1¼	**cups whole wheat flour**
¾	**cup unbleached white flour**
1	**tablespoon baking powder**
1	**teaspoon ground cinnamon**
1	**teaspoon ground allspice**
½	**teaspoon ground nutmeg**
¼	**teaspoon ground ginger**
1	**cup dried apples, finely chopped**
1	**cup nuts, chopped.**
5. Add the flour mixture to the liquid mixture, barely combining them. Do not beat.
6. Spoon the batter into the baking cups.
7. Bake at 375°F for 30 minutes, or until browned.

Banana Muffins

1. Preheat oven to 400°F.
2. Line muffin tins with:

   Paper baking cups.
3. Mix together in a large bowl:

1	cup whole wheat flour
1	cup unbleached white flour
2	tablespoons wheat germ
1	tablespoon baking powder
¼	teaspoon ground cinnamon.

4. Beat together in a medium bowl:

1	egg
4	medium-sized ripe bananas, mashed
¼	cup honey
3	tablespoons soy or corn oil
½	cup nuts, coarsely chopped, or ⅓ cup raisins.

5. Add the liquid ingredients to the dry ones, barely combining them. Do not beat. Spoon the batter into the baking cups.
6. Bake at 400°F for 10 minutes, then reduce heat to 325°F and bake 15 minutes longer, or until browned.

Crunchy-Top Whole Wheat Muffins

1. Preheat oven to 375°F.
2. Line muffin tins with:

   Paper baking cups.
3. Beat together in a large bowl:

1	cup water
1	egg
2	tablespoons honey
2	tablespoons corn oil.
4. Mix together in a medium bowl:

1¾	cups whole wheat flour
¼	cup dry milk
1	tablespoon ground cinnamon
2	teaspoons baking powder.
5. Prepare topping. Mix together:

1	cup soft whole wheat bread crumbs
3	tablespoons brown sugar
3	tablespoons margarine
2	tablespoons whole wheat flour.

   Set aside.

6. Add the flour mixture to the water mixture, barely combining them. Do not beat. Spoon the batter into the baking cups.
7. Sprinkle the crumb topping over the muffins, pressing it into the batter.
8. Bake at 375°F for 15 minutes, then reduce heat to 325°F and bake for 10 minutes longer.

Corn Meal Muffins with Dates

1. Preheat oven to 425°F.
2. Line muffin tins with:

   Paper baking cups.
3. Mix together in a large bowl:

   ½   **cup whole wheat flour**
   ½   **cup unbleached white flour**
   ¾   **cup polenta (coarse corn meal)**
   ⅓   **cup oat or wheat bran**
   1   **tablespoon baking powder**
   ⅛   **teaspoon sea salt.**
4. Beat together in a medium bowl:

   1   **egg**
   1   **cup water**
   ¼   **cup dry milk**
   3   **tablespoons honey**
   2   **tablespoons corn oil.**

5. Add:

   8   **whole dates, coarsely chopped.**
6. Add the dates and the liquid ingredients to the dry ingredients, barely combining them. Do not beat. Spoon the batter into the baking cups.
7. Bake at 425°F for 10 minutes, then reduce heat to 325°F and bake 15 minutes longer, or until browned.

Oat Bran Muffins

1. Preheat oven to 350°F.
2. Line muffin tins with:

   Paper baking cups.

3. Beat together in a large bowl:

1½	**cups water**
½	**cup dry milk**
¼	**cup honey**
¼	**cup dark molasses**
¼	**cup soy or corn oil**
1	**egg.**

4. Mix together in a medium bowl:

1¼	**cups whole wheat flour**
½	**cup unbleached white flour**
¾	**cup oat bran**
¾	**cup wheat bran**
1	**tablespoon nutritional yeast or wheat germ**
2	**teaspoons baking soda.**

5. Add the dry ingredients to the liquid ones, barely combining them. Do not beat. Fold in:

¾	**cup nuts, coarsely chopped**
½	**cup raisins.**

6. Spoon the batter into the baking cups.
7. Bake at 350°F for 25 minutes, or until browned.

Oatmeal Muffins

1. Preheat oven to 350°F.
2. Line muffin tins with:

   Paper baking cups.

3. Beat together in a large bowl:

1	**cup water**
1	**cup rolled oats**
½	**cup honey**
½	**cup margarine, melted**
¼	**cup dry milk**
1	**egg.**

4. Mix together in a medium bowl:

¾	**cup whole wheat flour**
¼	**cup unbleached white flour**
1	**tablespoon oat or wheat bran**
1	**tablespoon baking powder**
½	**cup raisins.**

5. Add the dry ingredients to the liquid ones, barely combining them. Do not beat.
6. Spoon the batter into the baking cups.
7. Bake at 350°F for 25 minutes, or until browned.

Pan Dulce

Light, sweet yeast rolls.

1. Beat together in a large bowl:

    1 cup very warm water
    ¼ cup dry milk
    2 tablespoons (2 packages) active dry yeast
    ¾ cup brown sugar.

    Let stand in a warm place (unheated oven) for 20 minutes.

2. Beat in:

    1 whole egg plus 2 egg whites.

    Add and beat thoroughly:

    ½ cup margarine, melted and cooled
    ⅛ teaspoon ground cinnamon
    ⅛ teaspoon sea salt.

3. Stir in:

    3 cups whole wheat flour.

    Turn out onto a floured board and add very gradually:

    3½–4 cups unbleached white flour.

    Knead until smooth, about 8 minutes.

4. Let rise, covered, in a warm place for 50 minutes, or until double in bulk.

5. Oil a baking sheet.

6. Preheat oven to 375°F.

7. Punch down the dough. Divide it into 16 pieces.

8. Gently knead each piece into a round roll. Set the rolls on the oiled baking sheet.

9. Let the rolls rise, covered, in a warm place for 20 minutes.

10. Bake at 375°F for 10 minutes, then reduce heat to 325°F and bake for 20 minutes longer, or until browned.

Pumpkin Bread

1. Preheat oven to 350°F.
2. Oil a 9" x 5" loaf pan.
3. Beat together in a large bowl:

1	whole egg plus 1 egg white
1	cup honey
⅓	cup soy or corn oil
1	cup (8 ounces) puréed pumpkin, or other winter squash.

4. Mix together in a medium bowl:

1½	cups whole wheat flour
2	teaspoons ground cinnamon
1	teaspoon ground allspice
½	teaspoon baking soda.

5. Add the dry ingredients to the liquid ones, stirring just until blended. Stir in:

½	cup walnuts, coarsely chopped
6	dried apricot slices, diced.

6. Spread the batter in oiled loaf pan and bake at 350°F for 50 minutes, or until toothpick inserted in center comes out clean.

Banana Bread

1. Preheat oven to 350°F.
2. Oil and flour a 9" x 13" glass casserole dish.
3. Beat together in a large bowl:

1	whole egg plus 2 egg whites
1¼	cups honey
⅔	cup corn oil
⅔	cup water
4	ripe bananas, mashed.

4. Mix together in a medium bowl:

2	cups whole wheat flour
¼	cup dry milk
¼	cup wheat germ
1½	teaspoons baking powder
1	teaspoon baking soda.

5. Add the dry ingredients to the liquid ones, along with:

1	cup nuts, chopped.

6. Beat well, then pour into oiled and floured dish and bake at 350°F for 50 minutes, or until toothpick inserted in center comes out clean.

Swedish Breakfast Bread

1. Mix together in a saucepan, then scald:

    2   **cups water**
    ½   **cup dry milk.**

    Let cool to lukewarm, then beat in:

    2   **tablespoons (2 packages) active dry yeast**
    1   **whole egg plus 1 egg white**
    ¾   **cup honey**
    ½   **cup margarine, melted and cooled.**

    Let stand in a warm place (unheated oven) for 20 minutes.

2. Stir in:

    ½   **teaspoon cardamom seed, crushed**
    3½ **cups whole wheat flour**
    3½ **cups unbleached white flour.**

    Turn the dough out onto a floured board and knead until smooth, about 10 minutes.

3. Cover the dough and let rise in a warm place for 40 minutes, or until double in bulk.

4. Preheat oven to 375°F.

5. Oil a baking sheet.

6. Punch down the dough and gently knead into three round loaves. Place the loaves on the oiled baking sheet and let them rise, covered, in a warm place for 30 minutes.

7. Bake at 375°F for 10 minutes, then reduce heat to 325°F and bake for 20 minutes longer, or until browned.

Amphitheatre Lake Bread Pudding

1. Preheat oven to 325°F.
2. Beat together in a large bowl:

1	**whole egg plus 2 egg whites**
2	**cups water**
⅔	**cup dry milk**
⅓	**cup honey**

   Grated rind of 1 lemon

1	**tablespoon fresh lemon juice**
1	**teaspoon vanilla extract**
½	**teaspoon ground nutmeg**
⅛	**teaspoon sea salt.**

3. Stir in:

3	**cups whole grain bread, muffin, or cake cubes.**

4. Let stand for 10 minutes.
5. Oil a 9″ x 14″ glass casserole dish.
6. Pour the pudding into the casserole, and sprinkle it with:

1	**teaspoon ground cinnamon.**

7. Bake at 325°F for 40 minutes, or until firm.
8. Spread on plastic-covered trays and dehydrate for 4½ hours at 145°F.
9. To rehydrate, barely cover with water, boil, stir, and serve.

Noodle Pudding

1. Prepare:

   2 servings Fresh Pasta (see Chapter Seven) or use 4 ounces dried commercial noodles.

   Cook the pasta until it is barely tender, then drain it in a colander.

2. Preheat oven to 350°F.

3. Spread the cooked pasta in a shallow, oiled glass casserole dish.

4. Sprinkle the pasta with:

   ¼ cup raisins.

5. Spread over the pasta:

   Finely grated rind of 1 lemon
   1 cup (8 ounces) lowfat cottage cheese.

6. Whip in a blender, or beat in a bowl, using a wire whisk:

   1 whole egg plus 1 egg white
   1 cup water
   ⅓ cup dry milk
   3 tablespoons honey
   1 teaspoon ground cinnamon
   ½ teaspoon ground allspice
   ¼ teaspoon sea salt.

7. Pour the milk mixture over the pasta. Dot with:

   Margarine bits.

8. Bake at 350°F for 45 minutes, or until firm and browned.

9. Spread on plastic-covered trays and dehydrate for 5 hours at 145°F.

10. To rehydrate, barely cover with water, boil, stir, and serve.

Rice Pudding

1. Cook:

   2   servings Brown Rice (see Chapter Seven) omitting bay leaf.

2. Preheat oven to 350°F.
3. Spread the cooked rice in a shallow, oiled glass casserole dish.
4. Sprinkle the rice with:

   ¼   cup raisins
   1   teaspoon finely grated lemon rind.

5. Whip in a blender, or beat in a bowl using a wire whisk:

   1   whole egg plus 1 egg white
   1½ cups water
   ⅔   cup dry milk
   3   tablespoons honey
   1   teaspoon ground cinnamon
   ½   teaspoon ground allspice
   ¼   teaspoon grated nutmeg
   ¼   teaspoon sea salt.

6. Pour the milk mixture over the rice. Dot with:

   Margarine bits.

7. Bake at 350°F for 40 minutes, or until firm and browned.
8. Spread on plastic-covered trays and dehydrate for 5½ hours at 145°F.
9. To rehydrate, cover with water, let stand briefly, boil, stir, and serve.

Fresh Fruit Crisp

No sugar is needed to make this breakfast treat.

1. Preheat oven to 350°F.
2. Oil a glass casserole dish.
3. Place in the bottom of the dish:

   3 cups thinly sliced fruit, such as unpeeled peaches, apricots, plums, berries, or peeled apples.

4. Sprinkle with:

   Finely grated rind of 1 lemon.

5. Mix topping in a separate bowl:

   1½ cups rolled oats
   1 cup unsweetened shredded coconut
   ½ cup whole wheat flour
   2 tablespoons ground cinnamon
   2 tablespoons ground allspice
   1 teaspoon ground ginger.

Add:

   ¼ cup corn or soy oil.

Mix thoroughly.

6. Crumble the oat topping evenly over the sliced fruit. Press it down firmly. Pour evenly over the topping:

   Juice of 1 lemon
   ½ cup any fruit juice.

7. Bake for 30 minutes, or until fruit is tender and topping is browned.
8. Spread on plastic-covered trays and dehydrate for 5 hours at 145°F.
9. To rehydrate, barely cover with water, boil, stir, and serve.

CHAPTER THREE

Backpack Lunches

Baking Techniques

Your Own Brick Oven

Convert your oven into a brick oven by lining its bottom with firebricks, which are designed to withstand great heat. Firebricks can be purchased at building supply stores. Measure the interior of your oven; the bricks are sized about 9" x 4½" and are 2 inches high. Do not cover heating vents or elements.

Clean the bricks before using them by soaking them in 1 gallon of water mixed with 2 tablespoons of bleach, then scrub them in warm soapy water, and rinse thoroughly.

If you leave the bricks inside your oven permanently, it will operate more efficiently. In fact, a brick oven bakes superior breads, pizza, crackers, and cookies because the bricks' heat evenly browns the food so the breads are crusty and the cookies and crackers are crisp. You will need to preheat the oven for an extra 10 minutes, but you can turn off the oven 10–15 minutes before the food is cooked since the bricks retain heat.

Yeast

Store yeast in the refrigerator, well wrapped against moisture. To activate yeast, dissolve it in warm water. For active dry yeast, use 110°F water; for fresh or compressed yeast, use 85°F water. Water temperatures which are too low or too high will render the yeast inactive.

Oven lined with firebricks.

Kneading

Kneading yeast bread is a joyful experience; ask your family and friends to take a turn. Knead dough on a surface that is slightly lower than your waist. Using your whole upper body, lean into the dough. Press the dough with your fists; keep your wrists straight. Fold the dough in half, give it a quarter turn, and press again. When the dough feels sticky, sprinkle it with a couple of tablespoons of flour at a time.

Rising

Yeast bread needs a warm, draft-free environment, such as an unheated oven, to rise properly. If you have a gas oven, the pilot light will provide just enough heat. For an electric oven, place a bowl of steaming hot water inside the oven, beneath or next to the dough.

Forming Rolls or Loaves

Roll the dough gently, sealing the bottom by pinching the seam. Put the bread in the pans with the seam side down. Squeeze air bubbles from loaves by pressing dough firmly into the pan.

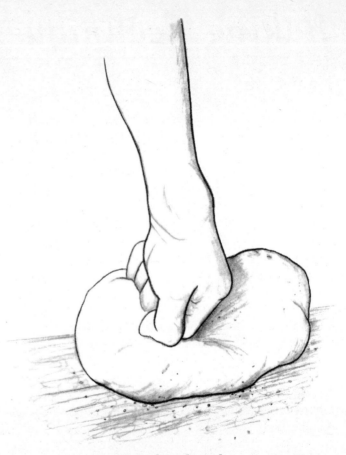

Kneading bread.

Storing

Turn bread out of pans and let it cool completely before packing and storing.

Crackers will keep several weeks; chapaties seven days; rye breads six days; and wheat breads, muffins, and tortillas three days.

Packing Crackers and Cookies

Save one-quart and half-gallon waxed milk cartons. Open the tops completely. Scrub and dry the cartons thoroughly.

To carry crackers, cookies, or pies, wrap individual servings in plastic wrap, then pack them tightly in the waxed cartons. Reclose the tops. Put the cartons inside large plastic bags.

When the cartons are empty, burn them, or flatten and pack them out.

Packing fragile foods in waxed milk cartons.

Basic Rolls or Bread

1. Beat together in a large bowl:

   3½   **cups very warm water**
   1   **tablespoon (1 package) active dry yeast**
   ½   **cup honey.**

   Let stand in a warm place (unheated oven) for 15 minutes.

2. Beat into the yeast mixture:

   ¼   **cup olive oil**
   ⅛   **teaspoon sea salt.**

   Add gradually:

   5   **cups whole wheat flour**
   3½   **cups unbleached white flour**
   ½   **cup wheat germ**
   ¼   **cup soya flour.**

3. Turn out onto a floured board and knead for 10 minutes, adding flour when necessary.

4. Replace dough in bowl, cover, and let rise in a warm place for 60 minutes, or until double in bulk.

5. Preheat oven to 375°F.

6. Oil two baking sheets, or two loaf pans.

7. Punch down the dough. For rolls, divide into 32 pieces, gently knead each piece into a ball, then flatten it. Place on oiled baking sheets. For loaves, divide in half. Gently knead into loaf shapes and pack firmly into oiled pans.

8. Cover and let rise in a warm place for 20 minutes.

9. Bake at 375°F—the rolls for about 35 minutes and the bread for about 50 minutes—until browned. The rolls and bread should sound hollow when tapped on bottom.

Irish Potato Bread

Fun to bake, and delicious.

1. Bring to a boil:

3	**cups water**
2	**medium potatoes, scrubbed but not peeled, quartered.**

   Simmer until tender. Drain the potatoes, reserving the potato water. Mash the potatoes.

2. Mix together in a large bowl:

2	**cups warm (not hot) potato water**
2	**tablespoons (2 packages) active dry yeast**
⅔	**cup honey.**

   Let stand in a warm place (unheated oven) for 20 minutes.

3. Add 1 cup of the mashed potatoes to the yeast mixture, along with:

½	**cup soy oil**
⅛	**teaspoon sea salt.**

4. Add gradually:

4	**cups whole wheat flour**
3	**cups unbleached white flour.**

   Turn out onto a floured board and knead well, about 10 minutes.

5. Replace dough in bowl. Cover and let rise in a warm place until double in bulk, about 70 minutes.

6. Preheat oven to 425°F.

7. Oil two 9″ x 5″ loaf pans.

8. Punch down the dough. Divide in half. Knead briefly and shape into loaves. Pack into oiled pans.

9. Cover and let rise in a warm place for 25 minutes.

10. Bake at 425°F for 15 minutes, then reduce heat to 325°F and bake for 35 minutes longer, or until loaves sound hollow when tapped on bottom.

Yeast Corn Rolls or Bread

1. Bring to a boil in a saucepan:

    1½ cups water.

    Gradually add, stirring constantly:

    ½ cup coarse corn meal.

    Simmer for 3 minutes, then turn off heat and let cool to room temperature.

2. Beat together in a large bowl:

    1½ cups very warm water
    2 tablespoons (2 packages) active dry yeast
    ⅓ cup honey.

    Let stand in a warm place (unheated oven) for 15 minutes.

3. Add the cooked corn meal, along with:

    ½ cup dry milk
    2½ cups whole wheat flour
    2½ cups unbleached white flour
    ¼ cup oat or wheat bran
    ½ teaspoon sea salt.

    Turn the dough out onto a floured board and knead until smooth, about 10 minutes, adding small amounts of flour when necessary.

4. Replace dough in bowl. Cover and let rise in a warm place for 70 minutes, or until double in bulk.

5. Preheat oven to 425°F.

6. Oil two baking sheets or two 9″ x 5″ loaf pans. Divide the dough into 32 pieces for rolls, or in half for loaves. Gently shape dough; place on or in pans. Cover and let rise in a warm place for 20 minutes.

7. Bake at 425°F for 20 minutes, then reduce heat to 325°F and bake rolls for 10 minutes longer or loaves for 30 minutes longer, or until bread is browned and sounds hollow when tapped on bottom.

Kitchen Sink Whole Grain Rolls or Bread

1. Mix together in a small bowl, then set aside:

   2   **cups warm water**
   ½   **cup bulgur (cracked wheat).**

2. Beat together in a large bowl:

   3   **cups very warm water**
   2   **tablespoons (2 packages) active dry yeast**
   ⅓   **cup honey.**

   Let rest in a warm place (unheated oven) for 15 minutes.

3. Drain the soaked bulgur and add it to the yeast mixture along with:

   1   **whole egg plus 1 egg white**
   1   **cup dry milk**
   ¼   **cup dark molasses**
   ¼   **cup soy or corn oil**
   ⅛   **teaspoon sea salt.**

4. Beat thoroughly and gradually add:

   4   **cups whole wheat flour**
   2   **cups rye flour.**

   Turn out onto a floured board and knead in:

   1   **cup triticale flour**

Three dozen rolls or two 9" x 5" loaves

   1   **cup gluten flour**
   ¼   **cup oat or wheat bran**
   ⅛   **cup soya flour**
   ⅛   **cup corn meal.**

5. Knead for 10 minutes, adding small amounts of flour when necessary.

6. Replace dough in bowl. Let rise in a warm place for 1 hour, or until double in bulk.

7. Oil two baking sheets or two 9" x 5" loaf pans, then sprinkle with corn meal.

8. Punch down the dough, then turn it out onto the floured board. For rolls, divide into 36 pieces, roll into smooth balls, and place on baking sheets, flattening them with your palm. For loaves, divide dough in half, shape into loaves, and pack into pans.

9. Preheat oven to 350°F.

10. Cover the bread. Let it rise in a warm place for 30 minutes.

11. Bake at 350°F. The rolls should bake for 35 minutes and the loaves for 50 minutes; both should be browned and sound hollow when tapped on bottom.

French Bread

1. Beat together in a small bowl:

    2¾ **cups very warm water**
    2   **tablespoons (2 packages) active dry yeast**
    ¼   **cup honey**
    2   **tablespoons olive oil.**

    Let stand in a warm place (unheated oven) for 20 minutes.

2. Mix together in a large bowl:

    4   **cups unbleached white flour**
    3   **cups whole wheat flour**
    3   **tablespoons wheat germ**
    ⅛   **teaspoon sea salt.**

3. Pour the liquid ingredients into the dry ones. Stir the dough, then turn it out onto a lightly floured board and knead for 2 minutes. Replace the dough in the bowl and let it rise in a warm place until double in bulk, about 1 hour.

4. Preheat oven to 425°F. Place a pie tin filled with water in the bottom of the oven.

5. Oil a 10″ x 15″ baking sheet.

6. Divide the dough in half. Gently roll into two long loaves, shaping them high and narrow (bread will flatten as it bakes). Place the loaves on the baking sheet.

7. Using a sharp knife, slash the loaves diagonally at 1-inch intervals. Cover the loaves with a damp cloth and let them rise in a warm place for 20 minutes.

8. Bake at 425°F for 15 minutes, then reduce heat to 325°F and bake for 35 minutes longer, or until loaves sound hollow when tapped on bottom.

Rye Bread

A good keeper.

1. Beat together in a large bowl:

> 1¾ cups very warm water
>
> 2 tablespoons (2 packages) active dry yeast
>
> ¼ cup molasses
>
> ¼ cup dark brown sugar.

Let stand in a warm place (unheated oven) for 20 minutes.

2. Add:

> 3 tablespoons olive oil
>
> 2 teaspoons caraway seed, crushed
>
> ⅛ teaspoon sea salt.

3. Stir in:

> 2 cups whole wheat flour
>
> 1 cup gluten flour.

Knead in very gradually:

> 2½ cups rye flour.

Knead the dough for 10 minutes, adding small amounts of additional flour when necessary.

4. Replace dough in bowl, cover, and let rise in a warm place for 70 minutes, or until double in bulk.

5. Oil a baking sheet.

6. Preheat oven to 350°F.

7. Punch down the dough, knead it briefly, and divide it in half. Shape into two round loaves.

8. Place the loaves on the baking sheet and let rise, covered, in a warm place, for 30 minutes.

9. Bake the loaves for 40 minutes, or until they sound hollow when tapped on bottom.

Italian Herb Rolls or Bread

1. Beat together in a large bowl:

   3½ **cups very warm water**
   1   **tablespoon (1 package) active dry yeast**
   ⅓   **cup honey.**

   Let stand in a warm place (unheated oven) for 15 minutes.

2. Beat into the yeast mixture:

   ¼   **cup olive oil**
   ⅛   **teaspoon sea salt.**

   Add gradually:

   4   **cups whole wheat flour**
   4   **cups unbleached white flour**
   1   **tablespoon vegetable seasoning (see Salt-Free Vegetable Seasoning, Chapter Seven) or use commercial**
   1   **cup gluten flour**
   1-2 **tablespoons dried Italian seasoning.**

3. Turn out onto a floured board and knead for 10 minutes, adding flour when necessary.

4. Replace dough in bowl, cover, and let rise in a warm place for 50 minutes, or until double in bulk.

5. Preheat oven to 375°F.

6. Oil two baking sheets, or two loaf pans.

7. Punch down the dough. For rolls, divide into 32 pieces; gently knead each piece into a ball, then flatten it. Place on oiled baking sheets. For loaves, divide in half. Gently knead into loaf shapes and pack firmly into oiled pans.

8. Cover and let rise in a warm place for 20 minutes.

9. Bake at 375°F. The rolls should bake for 30 minutes and the loaves for 40 minutes; both should be browned and sound hollow when tapped on bottom.

Onion Rolls

1. Beat together in a large bowl:

   3   cups very warm water
   2   tablespoons (2 packages) active dry yeast
   2   tablespoons honey.

   Let stand in a warm place (unheated oven) for 15 minutes.

2. Beat into the yeast mixture:

   3   tablespoons olive oil
   ¼   teaspoon sea salt.

3. Stir in:

   3   cups whole wheat flour
   3   cups unbleached white flour.

   Gradually knead in:

   1   cup gluten flour
   1   cup rye flour.

   Knead the dough for 10 minutes, adding small amounts of extra flour when necessary.

4. Replace the dough in the bowl. Cover and let rise in a warm place for 80 minutes, or until double in bulk.

5. Oil two baking sheets.

6. Mince:

   1   small onion.

7. Punch down the dough. Gently knead in half of the minced onion. Divide dough into 32 pieces. Shape into round rolls, then place them on baking sheets, flattening them with the palm of your hand.

8. Press the remaining minced onion into the tops of the rolls. Brush them with:

   Olive oil.

9. Preheat oven to 350°F.

10. Cover the rolls and let them rise in a warm place for 30 minutes.

11. Bake at 350°F for 40 minutes, or until browned.

Egg Bagels

1. Boil until tender, reserving water:

   3   medium potatoes, chopped

   2   cups water.

2. Beat together in a small bowl:

   1¼ cups potato water, cooled to lukewarm

   2   tablespoons (2 packages) active dry yeast

   ¼   cup honey.

   Let stand in a warm place (unheated oven) for 15 minutes.

3. Beat together in a large bowl:

   1   whole egg plus 2 egg whites (reserve yolks)

   4   tablespoons olive oil

   1   teaspoon sea salt.

   Add the yeast mixture, beat, then add:

   3   cups unbleached white flour

   1   cup whole wheat flour.

   Stir thoroughly.

4. Turn out onto a floured board and gradually add:

   1   cup unbleached white flour.

   Knead the dough for 10 minutes.

5. Replace the dough in bowl, cover, and let rise in a warm place for 75 minutes, or until double in bulk.

6. Punch down the dough, knead very briefly on a floured board, and cut into 18 pieces. Roll pieces into 7-inch long strands, then seal ends together, overlapping them firmly, like doughnuts.

7. Let the rolls rest on a floured board or counter for 15 minutes. Preheat oven to 425°F.

8. Bring to a boil in a large pot:

   3   quarts water

   2   tablespoons sugar.

9. Drop the bagels, three or four at a time, into the boiling water. When bagels rise to the surface, turn them and boil for 3 minutes longer.

10. Drain the bagels on cake racks, then place them on oiled baking sheets.

11. Brush the bagels with a glaze consisting of the 2 reserved egg yolks beaten with:

    3   tablespoons water.

12. Bake the bagels at 425°F for 25 minutes, or until well browned.

Big, Soft Bread Sticks

1. Beat together in a large bowl:

2	**cups very warm water**
2	**tablespoons (2 packages) active dry yeast**
¼	**cup honey**
1	**cup whole wheat flour.**

   Let stand in a warm place (unheated oven) for 15 minutes.

2. Stir in:

½	**cup dry milk**
2	**cups whole wheat flour**
⅛	**teaspoon sea salt.**

   Turn the dough out onto a floured board. Knead in gradually:

3	**tablespoons wheat germ**
2	**cups unbleached white flour.**

   Knead for 5 minutes.

3. Replace dough in bowl, cover, and let rise in a warm place for 40 minutes, or until double in bulk.

4. Preheat oven to 375°F.

5. Oil two baking sheets.

6. Punch down the dough. Divide into 16 pieces. Roll the pieces into 8-inch long sticks. Brush them with water and roll them in:

   Sesame seed.

   Place the sticks on the oiled baking sheets and let them rise, covered, in a warm place, for 20 minutes.

7. Bake at 375°F for 20 minutes, or until brown on bottoms.

Pita Bread

1. Beat together in a large bowl:

   2   **cups very warm water**
   3   **tablespoons (3 packages) active dry yeast.**

   Let stand in a warm place (unheated oven) for 15 minutes, then add gradually:

   ½   **teaspoon sea salt**
   5   **tablespoons olive oil**
   4–5 **cups whole wheat flour**
   1   **cup unbleached white flour**
   1   **tablespoon wheat germ.**

2. Mix thoroughly and knead for 10 minutes. Let rise, covered, in a warm place, for 90 minutes, or until double in bulk.

3. Punch down the dough, and invert bowl over it. Let rest for 30 minutes.

4. Punch down the dough again, divide into 9 pieces, and invert bowl over the pieces. Let rest for 30 minutes.

5. Preheat oven to 500°F.

6. On a lightly floured board, roll out the pieces to about 6½ inches in diameter. Place breads on ungreased baking sheets which have been sprinkled with:

   Coarse corn meal.

7. Cover breads with damp cloth towels and let rise for 30 minutes.

8. Bake at 500°F for 7 minutes, or until brown and puffy. Remove from baking sheet, wrap in cloth towel, and place inside a plastic bag. Do not let breads dry out or they will become too crisp.

9. To serve, cut in half and stuff each pocket with the filling of your choice, hot or cold: beans, meats, or raw or cooked vegetables.

10. To store for camping, wrap in aluminum foil, dull side out, then double-bag in plastic. Reheat, in foil, over stove or fire, or serve unheated.

Quick Wheat Crackers

1. Preheat oven to 325°F.
2. Oil baking sheets.
3. Mix together in a large bowl:

   > 1½   **cups whole wheat flour**
   > ½   **cup unbleached white flour**
   > 2   **teaspoons brown sugar**
   > 1¼   **teaspoons baking powder**
   > ⅛   **teaspoon sea salt.**

4. Cut in:

   > ½   **cup chilled margarine.**

5. Add:

   > 4   **tablespoons sesame seed.**

   Blend well, then add:

   > ⅔   **cup ice water.**

6. Blend well, then turn dough out onto floured board.
7. Roll dough as thinly as possible.
8. Cut the dough into 1″ x 2½″ rectangles. They needn't be even.
9. Place the crackers on oiled baking sheets. Prick them all over with a fork.
10. Bake at 325°F for 8–12 minutes, or until lightly browned on bottoms.

Quick Rye Crackers

1. Preheat oven to 325°F.
2. Oil baking sheets.
3. Mix together in a large bowl:

1	**cup rye flour**
½	**cup unbleached white flour**
½	**cup whole wheat flour**
2	**teaspoons brown sugar**
1¼	**teaspoons baking powder**
⅛	**teaspoon sea salt.**

4. Cut in:

½	**cup chilled margarine.**

5. Add:

2	**teaspoons caraway seed, crushed.**

   Blend well, then add:

⅔	**cup ice water.**

6. Blend well, then turn dough out onto floured board.
7. Roll dough as thinly as possible.
8. Cut the dough into 1″ x 2½″ rectangles. They needn't be even.
9. Place the crackers on oiled baking sheets. Prick them all over with a fork.
10. Bake at 325°F for 8–12 minutes, or until lightly browned on bottoms. These crackers brown very quickly; watch them carefully.

Whole Wheat Yeast Crackers or Bread

Two hundred and fifty crackers or two 9" x 5" loaves

No kneading is required.

1. Mix together in a large bowl:

   **2   tablespoons (2 packages) active
   dry yeast
   3   cups very warm water
   ½   cup honey.**

   Let stand in a warm place (unheated oven) for 15 minutes.

2. Mix together in a medium bowl:

   **6   cups whole wheat flour
   1   cup unbleached white flour
   ½   cup wheat germ
   ¾   cup dry milk
   ¼   teaspoon sea salt.**

3. Add to the yeast mixture:

   ¼   cup soy or corn oil.

   Then add the flour mixture to the yeast mixture.

4. Beat, then mix briefly with your hands.

5. Preheat oven to 375°F.

6. For crackers: Divide dough into 16 chunks. Roll out each chunk as thinly as possible, then sprinkle it liberally with **sesame seed.** Roll the seed into the dough. Cut dough into 1" x 2" rectangles. Place crackers on oiled baking sheet, and prick them generously with a fork. Bake for 5–8 minutes, or until lightly browned.

7. For bread: Divide dough in half. Pack firmly into two oiled 9" x 5" loaf pans. Cover and let rise in a warm place for 30 minutes. Bake for 45–50 minutes or until loaves sound hollow when tapped on bottom.

Oatmeal Crackers or Bread

1. Place in a large bowl:

    2 cups rolled oats
    2 tablespoons corn oil
    2 tablespoons dark molasses
    2 tablespoons honey.

2. Pour over the above mixture:

    2 cups boiling water.

    Stir, then cool to room temperature.

3. Mix together in a medium bowl:

    ½ cup very warm water
    1 tablespoon (1 package) active dry yeast
    Few grains sugar
    Few grains sea salt.

    Let stand in a warm place (unheated oven) for 15 minutes.

4. Combine yeast and oat mixtures.

5. Knead in gradually:

    2 cups whole wheat flour
    1½ cups unbleached white flour
    1 cup gluten flour.

    Knead for 8 minutes, or until smooth.

6. Let rise, covered, in a warm place, for 70 minutes, or until double in bulk.

7. Punch down the dough and knead briefly.

8. Preheat oven to 350°F.

9. For crackers: Divide dough into 16 chunks. Roll out each chunk as thinly as possible, then sprinkle it liberally with **sesame seed**. Roll the seed into the dough. Cut dough into 1" x 2½" rectangles. Place crackers on oiled baking sheet, and prick them generously with a fork. Bake for 15 minutes, or until lightly browned on bottoms.

10. For bread: Divide dough in half. Pack firmly into two oiled 9" x 5" loaf pans. Cover and let rise in a warm place for 30 minutes. Bake for 45–50 minutes, or until loaves sound hollow when tapped on bottom.

Wheat Chapaties

Flat breads that pack well.

1. Combine in a medium bowl:

1½	**cups whole wheat flour**
½	**cup unbleached white flour**
¼	**teaspoon sea salt**
¼	**teaspoon paprika.**

2. Cut in:

4	**teaspoons chilled margarine.**

3. Add very slowly, mixing to form a soft dough:

½–⅔	**cup ice water.**

4. Cover and let stand for 1 hour.
5. Heat griddle to medium.
6. Knead the chapati dough well, and divide it into 12 pieces.
7. On a floured board, roll out the chapaties as thinly as possible into rough circles about 7 inches in diameter.
8. Bake on griddle, turning them frequently, until very light brown.
9. To pack for traveling, allow them to cool completely. Cover with foil and wrap in plastic bags. Heat, wrapped in foil, over stove or campfire, or serve unheated.

Soy Chapaties

1. Combine in a medium bowl:

   1   cup whole wheat flour
   ½   cup unbleached white flour
   ½   cup soya flour
   ¼   teaspoon sea salt
   ¼   teaspoon paprika.

2. Cut in:

   3   teaspoons chilled margarine.

3. Add very slowly, mixing to form a soft dough:

   ½–1   cup ice water.

4. Cover and let stand for 1 hour.

5. Heat griddle to medium.

6. Knead the chapati dough well, and divide it into 12 pieces.

7. On a floured board, roll out the chapaties as thinly as possible, into rough circles about 7 inches in diameter.

8. Bake on griddle, turning them frequently, until very light brown.

9. To pack for traveling, allow them to cool completely. Cover with foil and wrap in plastic bags. Heat, wrapped in foil, over stove or campfire, or serve unheated.

Sesame Seed Chapaties

1. Brown in a cast-iron skillet until pale golden:

   2   tablespoons sesame seed.
2. Combine in a medium bowl:

   1   cup whole wheat flour
   1   cup unbleached white flour
   ¼   teaspoon sea salt
   ¼   teaspoon paprika.

   Add the toasted sesame seed.
3. Cut in:

   4   teaspoons chilled margarine.
4. Add very slowly, mixing to form a soft dough:

   ½–⅔   cup ice water.
5. Cover and let stand for 1 hour.
6. Heat griddle to medium.

7. Knead the chapati dough well, and divide it into 12 pieces.
8. On a floured board, roll out the chapaties as thinly as possible, into rough circles about 7 inches in diameter.
9. Bake on griddle, turning them frequently, until very light brown.
10. To pack for traveling, allow them to cool completely. Cover with foil and wrap in plastic bags. Heat, wrapped in foil, over stove or campfire, or serve unheated.

Oven-Baked Bannock Bread

A good keeper.

1. Preheat oven to 325°F. Oil an 8-inch square pan.
2. Mix together in a large bowl:

2½	**cups whole wheat flour**
1	**cup oat flour (rolled oats ground fine in blender)**
½	**cup nuts, chopped**
¼	**cup oat or wheat bran**
¼	**cup sesame seed**
⅛	**cup sunflower seed**
¼	**cup dry milk**
1	**teaspoon baking powder**
½	**teaspoon baking soda.**

3. Beat together in a medium bowl:

1	**cup water**
½	**cup brown sugar**
½	**cup honey**
½	**cup corn oil**
⅓	**cup dark molasses.**

4. Add the liquid ingredients to the dry ones. Mix thoroughly.
5. Spread the batter in the oiled pan and bake for 55 minutes, or until toothpick inserted in center comes out clean.
6. Cut the bread into individual servings, then cool and dry them on cake racks overnight. Wrap servings individually in plastic wrap, then store in plastic bags.

McGill Canyon Gingerbread

Goes well with cheese.

1. Preheat oven to 350°F.
2. Beat together in a large bowl:

1	whole egg plus 1 egg white
1	cup dark molasses
¾	cup honey
½	cup soy oil.

3. Mix together in a cup:

1	tablespoon baking soda
1	tablespoon hot water.

4. Mix together in a medium bowl:

3	cups whole wheat flour
3	tablespoons oat or wheat bran
3	teaspoons ground cinnamon
2	teaspoons ground ginger
1	teaspoon ground nutmeg
½	teaspoon ground cloves
⅛	teaspoon sea salt.

5. Mix together in a small bowl:

1	cup water
¼	cup dry milk
1	teaspoon vinegar.

6. Oil a 9″ x 13″ glass casserole dish.
7. Add the flour mixture to the egg mixture, alternately with the milk mixture. Add the baking soda. Beat well.
8. Stir in:

½	cup nuts, chopped, or ½ cup raisins.

9. Pour batter into the oiled dish and bake for 35–40 minutes, or until toothpick inserted in center comes out clean.

Cottage Cheese Bread

1. Preheat oven to 375°F.
2. Beat together in a large bowl:

   ¼   **cup corn or soy oil**
   ¼   **cup honey.**

   Add:

   1   **whole egg plus 1 egg white**
   1   **cup (8 ounces) small curd lowfat cottage cheese.**

   Beat well.
3. Mix together in a medium bowl:

   2   **cups whole wheat flour**
   3   **teaspoons baking powder**
   ½   **teaspoon baking soda.**
4. Oil and flour an 8-inch round cake pan.

5. Add the flour mixture to the liquid mixture, alternately with:

   ½   **cup nonfat milk.**

   Beat well.
6. Turn the batter into the prepared pan and bake at 375°F for 10 minutes, then reduce heat to 350°F and bake for 30 minutes longer, or until toothpick inserted in center comes out clean.

Dijon Mustard

1. Combine in a saucepan:

1½	**cups dry white wine**
½	**cup water**
1	**medium onion, chopped**
3	**cloves garlic, minced**
1	**whole bay leaf.**

   Bring to a boil, then simmer for 8 minutes. Pour into a bowl and let cool.

2. Place in a saucepan:

1¼	**cups dry mustard.**

   Slowly strain the wine mixture into the mustard, beating constantly.

3. Add:

1	**tablespoon honey**
1	**tablespoon olive oil**
½	**teaspoon sea salt**
	Dash of cayenne pepper.

   Heat slowly; simmer, stirring constantly, until thick. Mustard will continue to thicken as it cools.

4. Let cool, then pour into carefully scrubbed glass jars. Label and refrigerate.

5. Mustard will be mellow and very tasty after two to four weeks. It can be stored, refrigerated, for six months. Mustard can be carried in your knapsack for one to two weeks.

Pub Mustard

1. Combine in a saucepan:

    1½   **cups dark beer**
    ½   **cup water**
    1   **medium onion, chopped**
    2   **cloves garlic, minced**
    ½   **teaspoon ground cinnamon**
    ½   **teaspoon ground allspice**
    ¼   **teaspoon ground turmeric.**

    Bring to a boil, then simmer for 8 minutes. Pour into a bowl and let cool.

2. Place in a saucepan:

    1¼   **cups dry mustard.**

    Slowly strain the beer mixture into the mustard, beating constantly.

3. Add:

    3   **tablespoons brown sugar**
    ½   **teaspoon sea salt**
    Dash of cayenne pepper.

    Heat slowly; simmer, stirring constantly, until thick. Mustard will continue to thicken as it cools.

4. Let cool, then pour into carefully scrubbed glass jars. Label and refrigerate.

5. Mustard will be mellow and very tasty after two to four weeks. It can be stored, refrigerated, for six months. Mustard can be carried in your knapsack for one to two weeks.

Beef Jerkies

Tamari Beef Jerky

One cup of beef jerky pieces

1. Place in freezer until partially frozen:
    1   pound lean flank or round steak.
2. Remove and discard fat.
3. Slice the meat into ¼-inch thick strips, or less.
4. Mix together in a glass casserole dish:
    4   tablespoons tamari soy sauce
    1   tablespoon brown sugar
    2   teaspoons freshly ground black pepper
    Dash of cayenne pepper.
5. Marinate the beef strips in the sauce, stirring to coat, for 3 minutes.
6. Lay the beef strips directly on drying trays and dehydrate for 6 hours at 145°F.

Ranch Beef Jerky

One cup of beef jerky pieces

1. Place in freezer until partially frozen:
    1   pound lean flank or round steak.
2. Remove and discard fat.
3. Slice the meat into ¼-inch thick strips, or less.
4. Mix together in a glass casserole dish:
    4   tablespoons Worcestershire sauce
    1   tablespoon chili powder
    2   cloves garlic, minced.
5. Marinate the beef strips in the sauce, stirring to coat, for 3 minutes.
6. Lay the beef strips directly on drying trays and dehydrate for 6 hours at 145°F.

Fish Snacks

Tamari Fish Jerky

One cup of fish jerky pieces

1. Mix together in a glass casserole dish:

    ½   **cup tamari soy sauce**

    ½   **cup water.**

2. Wash and drain:

    1   **pound any uncooked fish fillets.**

3. Slice the fish as thinly as possible. Marinate the fish slices in the soy sauce for 15 minutes.

4. Pour the fish into a strainer. Rinse with cold water, then drain.

5. Spread the fish slices on clean paper bags. Let dry briefly.

6. Lay the fish slices directly on drying trays and dehydrate for 4½ hours at 145°F.

Tuna Treat

One-half to one cup of tuna snacks

Very fast and easy.

1. Drain in a sieve:

    1   **6½-ounce can Albacore or Bonita packed in water.**

2. Turn out onto a paper towel and pat dry.

3. Separate tuna into small flakes, and place them directly on drying trays.

4. Dehydrate at 145°F for 1 hour and 45 minutes.

Bean Sprouts to Go

1. Four days before your trip, rinse in a strainer:

   ¼ **cup alfalfa seed.**

   Place the seed in a bowl. Cover with warm water, and let stand in a warm place (on top of water heater or near oven pilot light) overnight.

2. Replace seed in strainer. Rinse and drain the seed. Wet a Turkish hand towel with warm water, then wring it thoroughly. Cover a large plate with half of the towel. Spread seed over the towel-covered plate. Fold the other half of the towel over the seed. Put the plate in a tightly-sealed plastic bag and keep it in a warm place overnight.

3. Next day, repeat step 2, rinsing the seed and rewetting the towel.

4. On the day you leave, rinse the sprouts, then wrap them in several thicknesses of paper towels. Double-bag the paper-towel-wrapped sprouts in plastic. The sprouts are a living food; they'll continue to grow as you travel. Keep them slightly moist.

Packing Raw Vegetables and Cheese

These fresh foods travel well.

Carrots

Scrub but don't peel. Cut into sticks. Will keep for 10 days.

Celery

Scrub. Cut into sticks. Will keep for five days.

Bell Peppers

Wash. Leave whole. Will keep for three days.

Small Cucumbers

Lemon cucumbers are best. Wash. Leave whole. Will keep for three days.

The day before you leave on your trip, prepare vegetables. After cutting carrots and celery into sticks, put them in a bowl of ice water and refrigerate overnight. Drain them well, then wrap them in paper towels. Double-bag towel-wrapped vegetables in plastic bags.

Processed Cheese

Select individual foil-wrapped or wax-covered portions of approximately 1 ounce each. Double-bag in plastic. These cheeses keep well without refrigeration for two weeks.

Natural Cheese

Select a hard cheese such as aged Cheddar. Dip a piece of cheesecloth in a mixture of 5 parts water to 1 part white vinegar; wring thoroughly. Wrap cheese in plastic wrap, then wrap with the dampened cheesecloth. Double-bag in plastic. Natural cheeses will keep without refrigeration for one week.

CHAPTER FOUR

Backpack Main Meals

Tamale Pie

A spicy treat.

1. Cook:

> 4 servings Polenta (see Chapter Seven).

2. Sauté for 10 minutes over high heat in a cast-iron Dutch oven:

> 1 tablespoon olive oil
> 1 onion, finely chopped
> 1 cup fresh whole mushrooms, finely chopped.

Lower heat to medium and add:

> 1 bell pepper, finely chopped
> 1 clove garlic, minced
> ¾ cup Thick Tomato Sauce (see Chapter Seven) or use commercial sauce
> 1 cup whole corn kernels, fresh, or canned and drained
> ¾ cup drained black olives, minced
> 1 tablespoon hot sauce, or to taste

> ½ cup bean stock or water
> 1½ cups cooked, drained pinto beans (see To Cook Dried Beans, Chapter Seven) or use 1 15-ounce can of beans, drained
> ⅛ teaspoon dried cumin, crushed.

3. Simmer, covered, for 30 minutes, then turn off heat and add:

> 2 cups grated cheese, such as mozzarella or Monterey Jack.

4. Combine polenta with bean mixture.

5. Spread on plastic-covered trays and dehydrate for 6 hours at 145°F.

6. To rehydrate, cover with water, let stand briefly, boil, stir, and serve.

White Bean Curry

1. Cook:

    1   cup dried white beans, such as great northern, navy, or black-eyed peas (see To Cook Dried Beans, Chapter Seven) or use 2 cups cooked, drained white beans, liquid reserved.

2. Heat in large cast-iron Dutch oven over high heat:

    2   tablespoons olive oil.

Add and sauté for 2 minutes:

    1   onion, finely chopped.

Then add, reduce heat to medium, and cook for 15 minutes:

    1   cup whole fresh mushrooms, washed and finely chopped

    1   tart apple, washed and cored but not peeled, finely chopped

    1   cup nuts, chopped.

3. Add:

    ¼   teaspoon cayenne pepper

    ⅛   teaspoon turmeric

    ⅛   teaspoon ground ginger

    ¼   teaspoon sea salt

    1   cup tomato sauce (see Thick Tomato Sauce, Chapter Seven) or use commercial sauce

    ¾   cup bean juice, stock, or water

    ½   cup raisins.

Add the 2 cups cooked, drained white beans.

4. Simmer for 30 minutes, then add:

    Juice of 1 lemon.

5. Spread on plastic-covered trays and dehydrate for 5 hours at 145°F.

6. To rehydrate, cover with water, boil, stir, and serve.

7. Serve with chapaties or crackers (see Index).

Chili Mac

Everyone's favorite.

1. Cook:

    ⅝ cup dried pinto beans (see To Cook Dried Beans, Chapter Seven) or use 1¼ cups cooked, drained, canned pinto beans.

2. Prepare:

    2 cups Thick Tomato Sauce (see Chapter Seven) or use commercial sauce.

3. Prepare:

    4 servings Fresh Pasta (see Chapter Seven) or use 12 ounces dried commercial pasta, such as elbow macaroni or rotelle spirals.

    Cook the pasta and drain it in a colander.

4. Grind in blender:

    3 whole seeded jalapeño chilies, fresh or canned

    5 ounces Hebrew National salami, coarsely chopped (optional).

5. Combine all of the above ingredients in a large saucepan. Heat to just boiling. Correct seasoning if necessary.

6. Spread on plastic-covered trays and dehydrate for 5 hours at 145°F.

7. To rehydrate, cover with water, boil, stir, and serve.

Lima Bean, Potato, and Sausage Casserole

Serves 4

1. Cook:

    1   cup dried lima beans (see To Cook Dried Beans, Chapter Seven) or use 2½ cups cooked, drained, canned lima beans.

Reserve liquid.

2. Heat in a cast-iron Dutch oven over high heat:

    3   tablespoons olive oil.

When the oil is hot, add and sauté for 5 minutes:

    1   onion, finely chopped
    5   small new potatoes, scrubbed but not peeled, finely chopped
    1   cup whole fresh mushrooms, finely chopped.

3. Reduce heat to medium and add:

    5   small sausages, cut into ¼-inch crosswise slices—choose any meat sausage, or TVP (vegetable) sausage, available in frozen food section of market.

4. When vegetables and sausages are browned, after about 10 minutes, reduce heat to low and add:

    1   clove garlic, minced
    1   cup Thick Tomato Sauce (see Chapter Seven) or use commercial sauce
    ¾   cup bean juice
    1   tablespoon Worcestershire sauce
    1   teaspoon dried mustard
    1   teaspoon fresh or ½ teaspoon dried tarragon

Sea salt to taste.

Add the cooked lima beans and simmer for 10 minutes.

5. Spread on plastic-covered trays and dehydrate for 5 hours at 145°F.

6. To rehydrate, cover with water, boil, stir, and serve.

Chili Beans

1. Heat a large cast-iron Dutch oven over high heat, then add:

    2   **tablespoons olive oil.**

    When oil is hot, add and sauté until lightly browned:

    1   **onion, finely chopped.**

    Add and sauté briefly:

    1   **medium bell pepper, minced.**

2. When pepper is soft, add:

    2   **cloves garlic, minced**
    ½   **teaspoon cayenne pepper**
    5   **tablespoons chili powder**
    1   **tablespoon dried or 2 tablespoons fresh oregano**
    1   **tablespoon whole dried cumin, crushed**
    ¼   **cup masa harina (corn flour), or whole wheat flour**
    ¾   **cup Thick Tomato Sauce (see Chapter Seven) or use commercial sauce**
    3¾   **cups cooked, drained pinto beans (see To Cook Dried Beans, Chapter Seven) or use canned beans**
    ½   **cup bean juice**
    Sea salt to taste.

3. Simmer until very thick, about 30 minutes, then turn off heat and add:

    1   **cup grated cheese, such as Parmesan or Dry Jack.**

4. Spread on plastic-covered trays and dehydrate for 4 hours at 145°F.

5. To rehydrate, cover with water, boil, stir, and serve.

6. Serve with crackers, chapaties, or tortillas (see Index).

Hashed Brown Potatoes with Lentils

1. Wash:

   1   cup lentils.

   Cover with:

   3   cups cold water.

   Boil, then reduce heat and simmer for 30 minutes. Drain in a colander.

2. Grate, then drain in a colander:

   6   medium-sized new potatoes, scrubbed but not peeled

   1   large onion.

   Wrap potatoes and onion in a cloth towel and squeeze out as much moisture as possible.

3. Heat a large cast-iron Dutch oven over high heat, then add:

   2   tablespoons olive oil.

   When oil is very hot, add the potatoes and onion. Fry thoroughly until very browned. Add:

   ½   teaspoon freshly ground black pepper

   Sea salt to taste.

4. Grind in a meat grinder, food processor, or blender:

   3–4 ounces salami (optional).

5. Combine lentils, fried potatoes, and salami. Add:

   Hot sauce to taste.

6. Spread on plastic-covered trays and dehydrate for 4½ hours at 145°F.

7. To rehydrate, barely cover with water, boil, stir, and serve.

Skedaddle Stew

1. Cook:

>   ¾   **cup dried soybeans (see To Cook Dried Beans, Chapter Seven).**

Reserve liquid.

2. Place in a cast-iron Dutch oven over high heat:

>   1   **tablespoon olive oil.**

When oil is hot, add:

>   1   **onion, minced**
>   7   **small new potatoes, finely chopped.**

When vegetables are light brown, reduce heat to medium and add:

>   2   **small zucchini, finely chopped.**

Sauté the vegetables until thoroughly browned, then add the cooked soybeans (about 1¾ cups) and:

>   1   **tablespoon whole wheat flour**
>   1   **cup reserved bean liquid**
>   1   **bell pepper, minced**
>   3   **ribs celery, minced**
>   3   **whole ripe tomatoes, chopped**
>   1   **clove garlic, minced**
>   2   **teaspoons fresh sage, minced, or 1 teaspoon dried**
>   1   **teaspoon sea salt**
>   **Cayenne pepper to taste.**

3. Reduce heat to very low and simmer, partially covered, for 30 minutes, adding more bean liquid if necessary.

4. Spread on plastic-covered trays and dehydrate for 6 hours at 145°F.

5. To rehydrate, cover with water, boil, stir, and serve.

Black Beans and Rice

1. Cook:

    1   **cup dried black beans (see To Cook Dried Beans, Chapter Seven).**

    Drain the cooked beans, reserving the liquid.

2. Cook:

    4   **servings Brown Rice (see Chapter Seven).**

3. Heat in a large cast-iron Dutch oven:

    2   **tablespoons olive oil.**

    When oil is hot, add:

    1   **onion, finely chopped.**

    Sauté the onion for 2 minutes, then add:

    1   **small zucchini, finely chopped.**

    Sauté until browned, then reduce heat and add:

    1   **bell pepper, finely chopped**
    2   **ribs celery, finely chopped**
    2   **cloves garlic, minced**
    2   **tablespoons fresh oregano, minced, or 2 teaspoons dried**

    ½   **teaspoon ground cumin**
    1   **whole bay leaf**
    1   **teaspoon dried mustard**
    1   **teaspoon sea salt.**

4. Add the beans (about 3 cups cooked beans) to the vegetables, along with:

    2   **cups bean liquid.**

    Bring to a boil, then simmer for 1 hour.

5. Remove from heat. Remove the bay leaf. Add:

    10   **sprigs fresh parsley or cilantro, minced**
    2   **tablespoons dry sherry.**

6. Combine the beans and rice. Spread on plastic-covered trays and dehydrate for 5½ hours at 145°F.

7. To rehydrate, cover with water, let stand briefly, boil, stir, and serve.

Vegetable Jambalaya

1. Cook:

   ⅝   **cup dried pinto beans (see To Cook Dried Beans, Chapter Seven) or use 1¼ cups any canned beans.**

   Reserve bean liquid.

2. Cook:

   4   **servings brown rice or couscous (see Brown Rice or Couscous, Chapter Seven).**

3. Heat a cast-iron Dutch oven over high heat. Add:

   1   **tablespoon olive oil.**

   When the oil is hot, add and sauté:

   1   **onion, minced.**

   When the onion is lightly browned, reduce heat and add:

   2   **whole ripe tomatoes, chopped**
   1   **bell pepper, minced**
   ¾   **cup chopped nutmeats**

   ½   **cup unsweetened shredded coconut**
   ¼   **cup dry white wine**
   2   **teaspoons fresh thyme, or 1 teaspoon dried**
   1   **teaspoon sea salt**
   Hot sauce to taste.

4. Add the cooked beans to the vegetable mixture, along with ½ cup bean liquid. Bring to a boil, then simmer gently for 30 minutes.

5. Combine the vegetable-bean mixture with the cooked rice. Correct seasoning if necessary.

6. Spread on plastic-covered trays and dehydrate for 6 hours at 145°F.

7. To rehydrate, cover with water, let stand briefly, boil, stir, and serve.

Ranch-Style Beans

1. Cook:

   1¼ cups dried pinto beans (see To Cook Dried Beans, Chapter Seven) or use 3¾ cups canned beans.

   Reserve the bean liquid.

2. Heat in a cast-iron Dutch oven over high heat:

   3 teaspoons corn or soy oil.

   When the oil is hot, add:

   1 onion, minced.

   When the onion is lightly browned, add:

   1 bell pepper, minced
   2 cloves garlic, minced
   3 tablespoons whole wheat flour
   2 tablespoons chili powder
   6 whole ripe tomatoes, chopped
   3 ribs celery, minced
   1 tablespoon fresh sage, or
   1 teaspoon dried
   1 teaspoon molasses
   2 whole cloves
   1 whole bay leaf.

3. Add the cooked pinto beans and enough of the reserved bean liquid to barely cover the beans and vegetables. Bring to a boil, then simmer, covered, about 45 minutes, or until thick.

4. Remove the cloves and bay leaf. Stir in:

   1 teaspoon sea salt
   Hot sauce to taste.

5. Spread on plastic-covered trays and dehydrate for 5½ hours at 145°F.

6. To rehydrate, cover with water, boil, stir, and serve.

7. Serve with crackers, tortillas, or chapaties (see Index).

Curried Lentils

1. Cook:

   1¼ cups dried lentils (see Lentils, Chapter Seven).

   Drain the lentils; reserve liquid.

2. Heat in a cast-iron Dutch oven over high heat:

   1 tablespoon soy or corn oil.

   When the oil is hot, add:

   1 onion, minced
   2 small new potatoes, scrubbed but not peeled, minced.

   Brown the vegetables, then reduce heat and add:

   1 teaspoon sea salt
   ½ teaspoon ground ginger
   ½ teaspoon curry powder
   ½ teaspoon turmeric
   ½ teaspoon dried ground chile peppers
   ¼ teaspoon ground cumin
   2 cloves garlic, minced.

3. Add the cooked lentils (about 3½ cups), along with enough reserved liquid to barely cover the lentils and vegetables.

4. Bring to a boil, then simmer for about 30 minutes, or until thick. Correct seasoning if necessary.

5. Spread on plastic-covered trays and dehydrate for 5½ hours at 145°F.

6. To rehydrate, barely cover with water, boil, stir, and serve.

7. Serve with crackers, chapaties, or pita bread (see Index).

Baked Soybeans

1. Cook:

>   1½ **cups dried soybeans (see To Cook Dried Beans, Chapter Seven).**

   Reserve liquid.
2. Preheat oven to 300°F.
3. Heat a cast-iron Dutch oven over high heat. Add:

>   1 **tablespoon soy or corn oil.**

   When the oil is hot, add:

>   1 **onion, minced.**

   When the onion is soft, add:

>   1 **bell pepper, minced**
>   4 **whole ripe tomatoes, finely chopped**
>   1 **tart apple, cored but not peeled, minced**
>   1 **tablespoon honey**
>   1 **tablespoon dry mustard**
>   1 **teaspoon sea salt**
>   **Cayenne pepper to taste.**

4. Add the cooked beans (about 3½ cups) to the vegetables, along with enough reserved bean liquid to barely cover the mixture. Correct seasoning if necessary.
5. Bake the beans at 300°F for 1½ hours. Stir occasionally and add liquid if necessary.
6. Spread the baked beans on plastic-covered trays and dehydrate for 5½ hours at 145°F.
7. To rehydrate, cover with water, boil, stir, and serve.

Spaghetti

1. Prepare:

   2 cups Thick Tomato Sauce (see Chapter Seven) or use commercial sauce.

   Add to the sauce:

   4 tablespoons hot sauce.

2. Prepare:

   4 servings Fresh Pasta (see Chapter Seven) or use 12 ounces dried commercial spaghetti, linguine, or fettucini.

   Cook the pasta and drain in a colander.

3. Grind in a meat grinder, blender, or food processor:

   3–4 ounces Italian dry salami (optional).

4. Combine tomato sauce, pasta, and salami in a large saucepan. Heat until just boiling.

5. Spread on plastic-covered trays and dehydrate for 5 hours at 145°F.

6. To rehydrate, cover with water, boil, stir, and serve.

Chilies Rellenos Casserole

A hearty dinner or breakfast.

1. Select two baking dishes, one of which fits comfortably inside the other.

2. Place 1 inch of water in the larger dish, and set it in the oven. Preheat oven to 325°F.

3. Thoroughly oil the smaller dish. Place in the bottom of the dish:

   ¼   **pound mild cheese, such as Monterey Jack, grated**

   1   **cup (8 ounces) lowfat cottage cheese.**

4. Beat together in a bowl:

   2   **whole eggs plus 4 egg whites**

   1½   **cups milk**

   5   **fresh jalapeño chilies (or 1 4-ounce can chilies, drained), seeds removed, and minced**

   2   **tablespoons whole wheat flour**

   5   **green onions, minced**

   1   **clove garlic, minced**

   ½   **teaspoon sea salt**

   ¼   **teaspoon ground cumin.**

5. Pour the egg mixture over the cheeses. Place the casserole inside the water-filled dish in the oven. Bake for 1 hour, or until toothpick inserted in center comes out clean.

6. Spread the casserole on plastic-covered trays and dehydrate for 6 hours at 145°F.

7. To rehydrate, barely cover with water, boil, stir, and serve.

Grain and Vegetables with TVP

1. Prepare:

   4   servings any grain (see Chapter Seven).

2. Prepare:

   4   servings Stir-Fried Vegetables (see Chapter Seven).

3. Add to the cooked vegetables:

   ½   cup TVP (Textured Vegetable Protein)

   1   cup bean liquid, stock, or water
   Hot sauce to taste.

   Let simmer for 3 minutes.

4. Combine the cooked grain with the cooked vegetables. Add:

   ¼   pound any well-flavored cheese, grated.

   Correct seasoning if necessary.

5. Spread on plastic-covered trays and dehydrate for 5 hours at 145°F.

6. To rehydrate, cover with water, let stand briefly, boil, stir, and serve.

Fried Rice

Best when made with rice which has been cooked, then chilled overnight.

1. Cook:

   4   **servings Brown Rice (see Chapter Seven).**

2. Cook:

   4   **servings Stir-Fried Vegetables (see Chapter Seven).**

3. When the vegetables are partially cooked, stir in the cooked brown rice. Allow the vegetables and rice to brown thoroughly, stirring occasionally.

4. Push the rice and vegetables to the sides of the pot, and add to the center:

   1   **teaspoon corn or soy oil.**

   When the oil is hot, break into it:

   2   **eggs.**

   Cook and stir the eggs until set, then mix with the rice and vegetables.

5. Turn off the heat and add, stirring well:

   1   **tablespoon salt-free seasoning (see Salt-Free Vegetable Seasoning, Chapter Seven) or use commercial**
   Soy sauce to taste
   Chopped green onions
   Chopped parsley.

6. Spread on plastic-covered trays and dehydrate for 5½ hours at 145°F.

7. To rehydrate, cover with water, let stand briefly, boil, stir, and serve.

Brown Rice with Nuts and Raisins

A sweet-sour dish.

1. Cook:

   4   servings Brown Rice (see Chapter Seven).

2. Heat a cast-iron Dutch oven or wok over high heat. Add:

   1   **tablespoon corn or soy oil.**

   When the oil is hot, add:

   1   **onion, minced.**

   When the onion is soft, add:

   1   **carrot, finely chopped.**

   When the vegetables start to brown, reduce heat and add:

   3   **leaves of cabbage, finely chopped.**

Sauté about 5 minutes more, then add:

    1¼   **cups water**
    1   **cup any unsalted nuts, chopped**
    ¾   **cup raisins**
    2   **tablespoons soy sauce.**

Cover and simmer for 1 hour.

3. Combine the cooked vegetables with the cooked rice.

4. Spread on plastic-covered trays and dehydrate for 6 hours at 145°F.

5. To rehydrate, cover with water, let stand briefly, boil, stir, and serve.

Spanish Rice

1. Wash and drain thoroughly in a strainer:

   1¾ cups raw brown rice.

   Turn the rice out onto a cloth towel and pat it as dry as possible.

2. Heat a cast-iron Dutch oven over high heat. Add:

   2   tablespoons olive oil.

   When oil is hot, add and sauté for 1 minute:

   1   large onion, minced.

   Reduce heat to medium and add the dried, raw brown rice. Cook and stir until lightly browned, then add:

   1   bell pepper, minced
   1   Anaheim chile, minced
   3   fresh whole tomatoes, chopped
   1   clove garlic, minced
   ½   cup TVP (Textured Vegetable Protein)
   1   teaspoon sea salt
   Cayenne pepper to taste.

3. Put the rice mixture in the top half of a double boiler, and pour over it:

   3   cups cocktail vegetable juice.

   Bring to a boil, then reduce heat and simmer for 50 minutes, stirring occasionally. When level of liquid falls below level of rice, place top half of double boiler over bottom half and complete cooking by steaming for 30 minutes, or until rice is tender.

4. Turn off heat and add:

   1   cup grated cheese
   10   sprigs fresh parsley, minced.

5. Spread on plastic-covered trays and dehydrate for 5¼ hours at 145°F.

6. To rehydrate, cover with water, let stand briefly, boil, stir, and serve.

Seafood Curry with Couscous

1. Heat in a large cast-iron skillet or Dutch oven:

   3 tablespoons olive oil.

   When hot, add:

   1 onion, finely chopped
   1 apple, cored but unpeeled, finely diced.

2. Sauté until lightly browned, then reduce heat and add:

   1 clove garlic, finely minced
   ½ cup unsweetened, grated coconut
   1 tablespoon curry powder
   ⅛ teaspoon cayenne pepper
   1½ cups milk.

3. When bubbling, add:

   ¾ pound firm white fish fillets.

   Simmer for 10 minutes, breaking up fish into small pieces, then add:

   5–6 ounces broken shrimp meats.

   Simmer a few minutes more.

4. Cook:

   4 servings Couscous (see Chapter Seven).

5. Combine couscous and curry mixture.

6. Spread on plastic-covered trays and dehydrate for 5 hours at 145°F.

7. To rehydrate, cover with water, boil, stir, and serve.

Shrimp Creole with Rice

For a special occasion.

1. Clean and finely chop, reserving skins and trimmings:

1	large onion
3	cups whole fresh mushrooms
3	ribs celery
2	cloves garlic.

2. Place the following in a stock pot with water, bring to a boil, then simmer for 1–3 hours:

   Vegetable trimmings (from step 1)
   Shells, heads, and tails of 1½ pounds
   uncooked shrimp.

   Drain, reserving liquid stock.

3. Prepare:

   4   servings Brown Rice (see Chapter Seven).

4. Preheat large Dutch oven over high heat. Add:

   3   tablespoons olive oil.

   When the oil is hot, add the chopped onion. Sauté for 3 minutes, then add the chopped mushrooms.

Sauté for 5 minutes, then reduce heat and add the chopped celery and garlic, along with:

2	tablespoons whole wheat flour
1	tablespoon oat or wheat bran
1	tablespoon fresh or 1 teaspoon dried basil
1	teaspoon fresh or ½ teaspoon dried thyme
½	teaspoon cayenne pepper.

5. Add 1 cup of the reserved stock, along with:

1	14½-ounce can peeled tomatoes.

   Bring to a boil, then simmer until thick, about 30 minutes, breaking up tomatoes into small pieces.

6. Add the cleaned shrimp and cook for 5–10 minutes more, breaking up the shrimp into small pieces.

7. Combine the brown rice with the shrimp mixture.

8. Spread on plastic-covered trays and dehydrate for 7 hours at 145°F.

9. To rehydrate, cover with water, let stand briefly, boil, stir, and serve.

Deviled Crab with Polenta

1. Preheat oven to 375°F.

2. Heat in a large cast-iron skillet:

   3   tablespoons margarine.

   Add and sauté briefly:

   1   cup minced scallions
   4   ribs celery, minced
   1   small bell pepper, minced.

3. Add:

   2   cups crabmeat, shelled and flaked
   3   tablespoons hot sauce
   2   tablespoons minced fresh parsley
   1   teaspoon dried mustard
   1   cup cracker crumbs
   Juice of 2 fresh lemons.

4. Mix thoroughly. Bake, in the cast-iron skillet, at 375°F for 30 minutes, or until lightly browned.

5. Cook:

   4   servings of Polenta (see Chapter Seven).

6. Combine polenta with deviled crab. Spread on plastic-covered trays and dehydrate for 5½ hours at 145°F.

7. To rehydrate, cover with water, let stand briefly, boil, stir, and serve.

New England Clam Chowder

1. Prepare:

> 20   fresh hard-shelled clams, or 1½ cups canned clams (2 6½-ounce cans).

To prepare hard-shelled clams, wash and scrub them thoroughly. Put them in a bucket with:

> 1   gallon cold water
> ¼   cup sea salt
> ¼   cup corn meal.

Let the clams stand for several hours, then rinse and drain them. Place in a large saucepan with:

> 4   cups water.

Bring to a boil, then simmer for 8 minutes. Drain the clams in a sieve, reserving the liquid. Remove meat from shells.

To prepare canned clams, drain them in a sieve, reserving the liquid.

2. Heat a cast-iron Dutch oven over high heat. Add:

> 3   tablespoons olive oil.

When the oil is hot, add:

> 1   large onion, minced.

Sauté the onion for 2 minutes, stirring constantly, then add:

> 10   small new potatoes, scrubbed but not peeled, minced.

Sauté the vegetables for about 20 minutes, or until they are brown. Reduce the heat as necessary.

3. Mince the clams; separate hard parts from soft parts.

4. Add to the sautéed vegetables:

> 2   tablespoons whole wheat flour.

Then add the hard parts of the minced clams, and the reserved clam liquid. Bring to a boil, then simmer for 30 minutes.

5. Add the soft parts of the minced clams to the chowder, along with:

> 2   cups milk
> 1   cup bottled clam juice
> 1   tablespoon butter or margarine
> ½   teaspoon sea salt
> ½   teaspoon freshly ground black pepper.

Simmer for 3 minutes.

6. Spread on plastic-covered trays and dehydrate for 5½ hours at 145°F.

7. To rehydrate, cover with water, boil, stir, and serve.

Bengali-Style Fish

1. Wash and drain:

   1   **pound fish fillets, about 1 inch thick.**

2. Chop and mix together in a small bowl:

   1   **large onion, minced**
   ½   **teaspoon grated ginger.**

   Spread the onion and ginger over the fillets. Set aside.

3. Heat a cast-iron Dutch oven over high heat. Add:

   2   **tablespoons olive oil.**

   When the oil is hot, add:

   1   **large onion, minced.**

   Stir-fry the onion until lightly browned. Reduce heat to medium-low.

4. Add to the fried onion:

   1   **teaspoon chili powder**
   1   **teaspoon honey**
   ½   **teaspoon ground turmeric**
   ¼   **teaspoon ground cloves**
   ¼   **teaspoon ground cardamom**
   3   **cloves garlic, minced.**

   Stir for 1 minute, then place the onion-covered fish fillets on top of the fried onions. Spread over the fish:

   2   **cups (16 ounces) plain lowfat yogurt.**

5. Cover the pot tightly. Cook for 10 minutes, or until the fish flakes easily.

6. Prepare:

   4   **servings of Bulgur Wheat (see Chapter Seven).**

7. Combine the cooked fish with the cooked bulgur. Spread on plastic-covered trays and dehydrate for 4½ hours at 145°F.

8. To rehydrate, cover with water, boil, stir, and serve.

Broiled Fish with Brown Rice Pilaf

1. Wash, then drain thoroughly in a strainer:

    1¾ cups raw brown rice.

    Turn the rice onto a cloth towel, and pat it dry.

2. Heat a cast-iron skillet over high heat. Add:

    3 tablespoons olive oil.

    When oil is hot, add and sauté for 1 minute:

    1 onion, minced.

    Reduce heat to medium; add brown rice with:

    1 cup whole fresh mushrooms, finely chopped.

    Cook and stir until lightly browned, then add:

    1 clove garlic, minced
    1 teaspoon sea salt
    ½ teaspoon freshly ground black pepper.

3. Place the rice in the top half of a double boiler. Add:

    2½ cups bean liquid, stock, or water.

    Bring to a boil, then simmer for 30 minutes.

4. Stir the rice. Place top half of double boiler over bottom half, and complete cooking by steaming for 45 minutes, or until rice is tender and fluffy.

5. Preheat broiler to highest setting. Wash and drain:

    1½ pounds of fish fillets.

    Measure the thickest part of the fish with a ruler. Cooking time will be 10 minutes for each measured inch of thickness.

6. Make a tray of aluminum foil, bending up the edges. Sprinkle onto the foil:

    1 tablespoon dry white wine.

7. Place the fish over the wine. Sprinkle over the fish:

    1 tablespoon vegetable seasoning (see Salt-Free Vegetable Seasoning, Chapter Seven) or use commercial
    1 tablespoon dry white wine.

8. Broil the fish, turning it once while cooking.

9. Mix the fish with the pilaf, flaking the fish and removing any bones.

10. Spread the mixture on plastic-covered trays and dehydrate for 5½ hours at 145°F.

11. To rehydrate, cover with water, let stand briefly, boil, stir, and serve.

Pasta Pesto

1. Prepare:

> **4 servings Fresh Pasta (see Chapter Seven) or use 12 ounces commercial dried pasta.**

2. Wash and drain:

> **4 cups fresh basil leaves.**

Place basil in blender, a small portion at a time, with:

> **½ cup light olive oil**
> **6 cloves garlic, peeled and halved**
> **4 ounces fresh Parmesan cheese, cut into small chunks**
> **2 teaspoons sea salt**
> **Small amount of water, if needed.**

3. Cook pasta until just tender, about 3 minutes for fresh pasta. Drain it quickly and replace in the saucepan. Pour pesto over pasta and stir constantly over very low heat just until cheese is melted and pesto is heated.

4. Spread on plastic-covered trays and dehydrate for 5½ hours at 145°F.

5. To rehydrate, barely cover with water, boil, stir, and serve.

Tofu Pasta Pesto

This is a lighter version of pasta pesto.

1. Prepare:

4	servings Fresh Pasta (see Chapter Seven) or use 12 ounces commercial dried pasta.

2. Wash and drain:

4	cups fresh basil leaves.

   Place basil in blender, a small portion at a time, with:

4	tablespoons olive oil
4	tablespoons water
½	pound raw tofu, rinsed and drained
4	cloves garlic, peeled and halved
3	ounces fresh Parmesan cheese, cut into small chunks
2	teaspoons sea salt
	Hot sauce to taste.

   Whirl in blender until smooth.

3. Cook pasta until just tender, about 3 minutes for fresh pasta. Drain it quickly and replace in the saucepan. Pour pesto over pasta and stir constantly over very low heat just until cheese is melted and pesto is heated.

4. Spread on plastic-covered trays and dehydrate for 5½ hours at 145°F.

5. To rehydrate, barely cover with water, boil, stir, and serve.

Pasta with Ricotta Cheese

1. Prepare:

   4 servings Fresh Pasta (see Chapter Seven) or use 12 ounces commercial pasta.

2. Cook pasta until just tender. Drain it quickly and replace it in the saucepan. Add:

   1 pound ricotta cheese
   ½ cup grated Parmesan cheese
   1 tablespoon butter or margarine
   3 green onions, minced
   6 sprigs parsley, minced
   1 teaspoon sea salt
   1 teaspoon freshly ground black pepper.

3. Heat over very low heat, stirring constantly, for 2 minutes.

4. Spread on plastic-covered trays and dehydrate for 5½ hours at 145°F.

5. To rehydrate, barely cover with water, boil, stir, and serve.

Pasta e Fagioli

1. Cook:

   1½ **cups dried white beans (see To Cook Dried Beans, Chapter Seven) or use 4 cups canned beans.**

   Reserve bean liquid.

2. Prepare and reserve:

   4 **servings Fresh Pasta (see Chapter Seven) or use 12 ounces commercial pasta.**

3. Heat a cast-iron Dutch oven over low heat. Add:

   2 **tablespoons olive oil.**

   When the oil is hot, add and sauté for 1 minute:

   2 **tablespoons fresh rosemary, minced, or 1 tablespoon dried**

   1 **clove garlic, minced.**

   Add:

   4 **whole fresh tomatoes, chopped.**

Add the cooked beans (4 cups), along with:

   3 **cups bean liquid**

   1½ **teaspoons sea salt**

   ¼ **teaspoon cayenne pepper.**

Bring to a boil, then simmer for 10 minutes.

4. Meanwhile, bring to a boil:

   2 **quarts water.**

Cook the pasta until just tender.

5. Add the cooked, drained pasta to the beans, along with:

   2 **ounces fresh Parmesan cheese, grated.**

6. Blend together. Correct seasoning if necessary.

7. Spread on plastic-covered trays and dehydrate for 5½ hours at 145°F.

8. To rehydrate, cover with water, boil, stir, and serve.

Pasta Primavera

Use very young, tender vegetables.

1. Prepare:

4	servings Fresh Pasta (see Chapter Seven) or use 12 ounces commercial pasta.

2. Bring to a boil in a large saucepan:

1	quart water.

3. Drop into the water and cook for 1 minute:

1	zucchini, chopped
8	green beans, sliced
1	cup broccoli flowerettes, separated.

    Rinse the vegetables under cold water and drain them.

4. Heat in a cast-iron Dutch oven over high heat:

2	tablespoons olive oil.

    When the oil is hot, add:

1	onion, minced
2	cups fresh whole mushrooms, thinly sliced.

When the vegetables are lightly browned, reduce heat to very low and add:

1	cup plain yogurt
2	cloves garlic, minced
4	tablespoons minced fresh basil, or 2 tablespoons dried
4	tablespoons minced fresh parsley
1	teaspoon sea salt

Cayenne pepper to taste.

Add the zucchini, green beans, and broccoli.

5. Cook the pasta until just tender. Drain in a colander.

6. Add the drained pasta to the vegetable mixture. Correct seasoning if necessary. Add:

¾	cup freshly grated Parmesan cheese.

    Stir and heat just until cheese is melted.

7. Spread on plastic-covered trays and dehydrate for 5½ hours at 145°F.

8. To rehydrate, cover with water, boil, stir, and serve.

Split Pea or Lentil Soup with Salami

Thick and hearty.

1. Wash and drain, then place in a large pot:

    1½ cups green or yellow split peas, or lentils.

2. Place the following vegetables in a blender, a small portion at a time. Cover with water and grind. After you grind each portion, add it to the pot of peas.

    1   carrot, scrubbed but not peeled, coarsely chopped

    2   ribs celery, scrubbed, coarsely chopped

    1   onion, quartered

    2   cloves garlic, peeled

    3   ounces any salami (optional)

    2   tablespoons fresh rosemary, or 1 tablespoon dried.

3. Add to the peas, water, and ground vegetables:

    ¼   cup TVP (Textured Vegetable Protein)

    1   teaspoon olive oil

    1   teaspoon honey

    1   whole bay leaf.

4. Bring to a boil, then reduce heat and simmer for 3 hours. Add water, 1 cup at a time, as needed.

5. Add and simmer for a few minutes:

    ¼   cup dry sherry

    3   tablespoons hot sauce

    ½   teaspoon freshly ground black pepper

    Sea salt to taste.

6. Remove and discard bay leaf. Spread the soup on plastic-covered trays and dehydrate for 6 hours at 145°F.

7. To rehydrate, cover with water, boil, stir, and serve.

Cream of Mushroom Soup

Fast and easy.

1. Heat a large cast-iron Dutch oven over high heat, then add:

   3   tablespoons olive oil.

   When oil is hot, add:

   1   onion, finely chopped
   6   cups fresh whole mushrooms, finely chopped.

2. Cook for 5 minutes, stirring occasionally, then reduce heat and add:

   3   ribs celery, minced
   1   clove garlic, minced
   ⅛   teaspoon ground nutmeg
   Dash of cayenne pepper
   4   tablespoons whole wheat flour
   Few grains sea salt.

3. Simmer, stirring, for 3 minutes, then add:

   ¼   cup dry white wine
   ¼   cup stock or water.

4. Cover and simmer for 10 minutes, then turn off heat and stir in:

   2   cups milk.

5. Spread on plastic-covered trays and dehydrate for 5½ hours at 145°F.

6. To rehydrate, cover with water, boil, stir, and serve.

7. Serve with crackers (see Index).

Corn-Potato Chowder

1. Heat a large cast-iron Dutch oven over high heat, then add:

   2   **tablespoons olive oil.**

   Add and sauté, stirring constantly, until transparent:

   1   **onion, finely chopped.**

   Add and sauté until lightly browned:

   5   **medium-sized new potatoes, scrubbed but not peeled, finely chopped.**

2. Reduce heat to medium, add and sauté for 3 minutes:

   5   **mushrooms, finely chopped.**

3. Add:

   2   **tablespoons soy or whole wheat flour**
   1   **rib celery, finely chopped**
   2   **cups water or stock**
   2   **cups whole corn kernels, fresh or canned, drained**
   1   **teaspoon fresh thyme, or ½ teaspoon dried**
   2   **cloves garlic, finely minced**
   ½   **teaspoon sea salt**
   ½   **teaspoon freshly ground black pepper.**

   Bring to a boil, then reduce heat to low, cover, and simmer for 30 minutes.

4. Add and heat:

   1   **tablespoon butter or margarine**
   1   **cup milk.**

5. Spread on plastic-covered trays and dehydrate for 6 hours at 145°F.

6. To rehydrate, cover with water, boil, stir, and serve.

Barley-Bean Soup

1. Cook:

   ¾ **cup dried kidney beans (see To Cook Dried Beans, Chapter Seven) or use 1¾ cups canned beans.**

   Reserve the bean liquid.

2. Wash, then drain thoroughly:

   ¼ **cup pearled barley.**

3. Heat a cast-iron Dutch oven over high heat. Add:

   1 **tablespoon corn or soy oil.**

   When the oil is hot, add:

   1 **onion, minced.**

   When the onion is soft, add the drained barley and:

   1 **cup mushrooms, finely chopped**
   1 **carrot, finely minced.**

   Sauté the vegetables until well browned, reducing heat as necessary.

4. Add to the cooked vegetables the cooked kidney beans, reserved bean liquid (enough to cover), and:

   2 **teaspoons fresh rosemary, minced, or 1 teaspoon dried**
   1 **teaspoon freshly ground black pepper**
   1 **teaspoon sea salt.**

5. Bring to a boil, then simmer the soup for 30 minutes, or until the barley is tender.

6. Spread on plastic-covered trays and dehydrate for 5½ hours at 145°F.

7. To rehydrate, cover with water, boil, stir, and serve.

Minestrone

Small amounts of many different vegetables give this soup its characteristic flavor.

1. Cook:

   ½ cup dried kidney beans (see To Cook Dried Beans, Chapter Seven) or use 1⅓ cups canned beans.

   Drain the beans in a colander, reserving the liquid.

2. Heat a cast-iron Dutch oven over high heat. Add:

   2 tablespoons olive oil.

   When the oil is hot, add:

   1 onion, minced.

   When the onion is soft, add:

   1 carrot, minced
   6 green beans, finely chopped
   1 small zucchini, finely chopped
   3 small new potatoes, scrubbed but not peeled, minced.

Sauté the vegetables, stirring occasionally, until they are thoroughly browned, then add the 1⅓ cups cooked beans, along with:

   3 cups reserved bean liquid
   4 whole tomatoes, chopped
   2 teaspoons fresh thyme, or 1 teaspoon dried
   2 teaspoons fresh oregano, or 1 teaspoon dried
   1 teaspoon fresh sage, minced, or ½ teaspoon dried
   1 teaspoon sea salt
   Dash of cayenne pepper.

3. Simmer the soup for 30 minutes, then add:

   ½ cup tiny soup noodles.

   Simmer for 10 minutes more.

4. Spread the soup on plastic-covered trays and dehydrate for 5½ hours at 145°F.

5. To rehydrate, cover with water, boil, stir, and serve.

CHAPTER FIVE

Backpack Snacks and Desserts

Chocolate or Carob Chip Cookies

Seven dozen cookies

1. Preheat oven to 325°F. Oil baking sheets.
2. Beat together in a large bowl:

   ½   cup margarine, softened
   1¼ cups brown sugar
   1   whole egg plus 1 egg white
   1   teaspoon vanilla extract
   1   teaspoon fresh lemon juice
   ½   teaspoon ground cinnamon.

3. Mix together in a medium bowl:

   1¼ cups whole wheat flour
   ¼   cup rolled oats
   1   teaspoon baking soda.

4. Add the flour mixture to the sugar mixture. Beat thoroughly. Stir in:

   2   cups (1 12-ounce package) semisweet chocolate or carob chips
   ½   cup nuts, chopped
   ½   cup unsweetened shredded coconut.

   Blend well.

5. Drop the batter by teaspoonful onto oiled baking sheets. Bake for 8 minutes, or until very light brown. Remove cookies from baking sheets immediately, while still soft.

123

Oatmeal Cookies

1. Preheat oven to 350°F.
2. Beat together in a small bowl:

1	whole egg plus 1 egg white
½	cup raisins
1	teaspoon vanilla extract
1	teaspoon finely grated lemon rind.

   Set aside.
3. Beat together in a large bowl:

½	cup corn oil
1	cup honey.

   Add:

1	cup whole wheat flour
¼	cup unbleached white flour
1	tablespoon oat or wheat bran
1	teaspoon ground cinnamon
1	teaspoon baking soda.

   Beat well.
4. Add the egg and raisin mixture to the flour mixture, along with:

1	cup rolled oats
1	cup nuts, chopped.

   Mix thoroughly.
5. Drop by teaspoonful onto ungreased baking sheets. Bake at 350°F for 10–12 minutes, or until very lightly browned.

Russian Tea Cakes

1. Preheat oven to 300°F.
2. Cream together:

½	**cup margarine**
3	**tablespoons brown sugar**
1	**teaspoon vanilla extract.**

3. Grind in a blender or meat grinder:

   1½ **cups pecans, almonds, or walnuts.**

4. Sift, then measure:

½	**cup whole wheat flour**
½	**cup unbleached white flour.**

5. Blend the flours into the margarine mixture. Add the ground nuts.
6. Oil a baking sheet.
7. Roll the dough into balls the size of small walnuts, and place them on the baking sheet.
8. Bake for 30 minutes, or until bottoms are lightly browned.
9. While the cakes are hot, roll them in:

   Sifted confectioners' sugar.

10. Replace the cakes on the baking sheet, and return them to the oven for 3 minutes.
11. Cool completely before wrapping the cakes individually in plastic wrap, and storing in plastic bags.

Sesame Seed Cookies

Delicious and nutritious.

1. Preheat oven to 350°F.
2. Brown in a cast-iron skillet over medium heat, stirring frequently:

1	**cup sesame seed**
¾	**cup unsweetened grated coconut.**

3. Beat together in a large bowl:

¾	**cup corn oil**
¾	**cup honey**
1	**egg**
1	**teaspoon vanilla extract.**

4. Mix together in a medium bowl:

1½	**cups whole wheat flour**
¼	**cup unbleached white flour**
¼	**cup soya flour**
½	**teaspoon baking powder**
½	**teaspoon baking soda.**

5. Add the flour mixture to the oil mixture. Beat thoroughly.
6. Blend in the toasted seed and coconut.
7. Roll the dough into balls the size of small walnuts and place them 2 inches apart on ungreased baking sheets. Dip a fork into cold water and use it to flatten cookies.
8. Bake at 350°F for 12 minutes, or until lightly browned.

Snickerdoodles

Cinnamon cookies with crinkled tops.

1. Cream together in a large bowl:

    ½   **cup margarine**
    ¾   **cup brown sugar.**

    Beat in:

    1   **egg.**

2. Mix together in a smaller bowl:

    1   **cup whole wheat flour**
    ⅔   **cup unbleached white flour**
    ½   **teaspoon baking powder**
    ½   **teaspoon baking soda**
    ½   **teaspoon ground nutmeg.**

3. Gradually add the flour mixture to the egg mixture.

4. Cover the dough and refrigerate for several hours.

5. Preheat oven to 400°F.

6. Roll the dough into balls the size of small walnuts. Roll them in a mixture of:

    1   **tablespoon brown sugar**
    1   **tablespoon ground cinnamon.**

7. Place the cookies 2 inches apart on ungreased baking sheets.

8. Bake for 8–10 minutes, or until lightly browned but still soft.

Ranger Cookies

Hearty oat cookies.

1. Preheat oven to 350°F.

2. Cream together in a large bowl:

½	**cup margarine**
½	**cup honey**
½	**cup brown sugar.**

   Beat in:

1	**egg**
½	**teaspoon vanilla extract.**

3. Mix together in a medium bowl:

½	**cup whole wheat flour**
½	**cup unbleached white flour**
½	**teaspoon baking soda**
½	**teaspoon baking powder**
½	**cup rolled oats**
½	**cup any nuts, chopped**
½	**cup unsweetened shredded coconut**
½	**cup whole wheat flakes cereal, or toasted rice cereal.**

4. Oil baking sheets.

5. Gradually add the dry ingredients to the liquid mixture.

6. Roll the dough into 1-inch balls, and place them 2 inches apart on the baking sheets.

7. Bake at 350°F for 10 minutes, or until lightly browned.

Peanut Butter Cookies

1. Preheat oven to 375°F.
2. Beat together in a large bowl:

   ½   **cup corn oil**
   1   **cup honey**
   1   **cup peanut butter**
   1   **egg**
   1   **teaspoon vanilla extract.**
3. Sift together in a medium bowl:

   1   **cup whole wheat flour**
   ½   **cup unbleached white flour**
   1   **tablespoon oat or wheat bran**
   1   **teaspoon ground cinnamon**
   ½   **teaspoon baking soda.**
4. Oil baking sheets.

5. Add the dry ingredients to the liquid ones. Blend.
6. Stir in:

   ½   **cup peanuts, chopped.**
   Blend thoroughly.
7. Roll the dough into balls the size of small walnuts.
8. Place the balls 2 inches apart on the baking sheets. Flatten the cookies with a fork.
9. Bake at 375°F for 12–14 minutes, or until lightly browned.

Old-Fashioned Vermont Ginger Cookies

1. Preheat oven to 350°F. Oil baking sheets.

2. Beat together in a large bowl:

¾	**cup molasses**
½	**cup corn oil**
½	**cup water**
½	**cup dark brown sugar**
¼	**cup dry milk**
2	**teaspoons ground cinnamon**
2	**teaspoons ground ginger**
2	**teaspoons baking soda**
1	**teaspoon cider vinegar**
⅛	**teaspoon sea salt.**

3. Add gradually, to form a soft dough:

   2½–3   cups whole wheat flour.

4. Turn the dough out onto a floured board. Roll into a rectangle, ¼-inch thick. Using a sharp knife, cut into 24 pieces.

5. Place the cookies on the baking sheets. Mark lightly with back of knife.

6. Bake for 15 minutes, or until cookies spring back when lightly touched.

Thumb Print Cookies

1. Beat together in a large bowl:

    ⅔   **cup margarine**
    ½   **cup brown sugar**
    1   **whole egg plus 1 egg white**
    1   **teaspoon vanilla extract.**

2. Sift together in a medium bowl:

    1¼   **cups whole wheat flour**
    1¼   **cups unbleached white flour**
    ¼   **cup wheat germ**
    1   **teaspoon baking powder.**

3. Add the dry ingredients to the liquid ones, beating thoroughly.

4. Cover the bowl of dough tightly and refrigerate it for several hours.

5. Preheat oven to 350°F. Oil baking sheets.

6. Roll the dough into balls the size of small walnuts. Place them on baking sheets.

7. Bake the cookies at 350°F for 6 minutes. Remove them from the oven. Using your thumb, or the back of a spoon, press a well into the center of each cookie. Return the cookies to the oven and bake for 7 minutes longer, or until light brown. Let them cool completely.

8. Fill the centers of the cookies with:

    Any fruit jam.

Fresh Fruit Bars

Sweet and rich.

1. Preheat oven to 350°F.
2. Mix together in a large bowl:

   1   cup whole wheat flour
   1   cup unbleached white flour
   ½   cup brown sugar
   ½   teaspoon baking powder.

   Cut in:

   ¾   cup chilled margarine.

   Add:

   1   whole egg plus 1 egg white, beaten.

   Press the dough mixture into a 9" x 13" oiled pan.

3. Prepare fruit filling.

   4   cups thinly sliced fruit—peeled apples or unpeeled peaches or apricots.

Mix the sliced fruit with:

   ⅓   cup honey
   ¼   cup whole wheat flour
   1   tablespoon ground cinnamon.

4. Spread the fruit filling over the dough mixture.
5. Prepare crumb topping. Blend together in a medium bowl:

   ½   cup brown sugar
   ½   cup whole wheat flour
   ½   cup margarine
   ½   cup whole wheat bread crumbs
   1   tablespoon ground cinnamon.

6. Crumble topping over the fruit filling.
7. Bake at 350°F for 50 minutes.
8. Let cool completely before cutting into bars.

Blueberry Bars

1. Preheat oven to 375°F.
2. Cream together in a large bowl:

   1½ **cups margarine**
   1¼ **cups dark brown sugar**
   1   **teaspoon vanilla extract.**

3. Gradually add:

   3   **cups whole wheat flour**
   1   **cup rolled oats**
   2   **tablespoons oat or wheat bran.**

4. Oil a 9" x 13" pan.
5. Firmly press half of the dough into the pan, forming a crust.
6. Bake for 10 minutes at 375°F.
7. Spread over the baked crust:

   2½ **cups unsweetened blueberry (or other fruit) jam.**

8. Crumble the rest of the dough evenly over the jam.
9. Bake 15 minutes longer at 375°F.
10. Let cool thoroughly before cutting into bars.

Fruit-Filled Bars

1. Combine in a saucepan:

   1½ **cups any dried fruit slices,
   chopped**

   1 **cup water.**

   Simmer for 15 minutes over low heat. Add:

   2 **tablespoons honey**

   1 **tablespoon fresh lemon juice.**

   Set aside.

2. Preheat oven to 350°F.

3. Beat together in a large bowl:

   ½ **cup honey**

   ⅓ **cup corn oil.**

4. Mix together in a medium bowl:

   1¼ **cups whole wheat flour**

   1 **cup rolled oats**

   ¾ **cup pecans, chopped**

   ¼ **cup wheat germ**

   3 **tablespoons oat or wheat bran**

   ½ **teaspoon baking soda.**

5. Gradually add the flour mixture to the honey mixture. Blend.

6. Oil an 8-inch square pan.

7. Spread half the oat mixture in the pan. Top with the fruit mixture. Crumble the remaining oat mixture over the top. Pat down.

8. Bake at 350°F for 30 minutes, or until browned.

9. Cool completely before cutting into bars.

Black Rock Desert Brownies

1. Preheat oven to 350°F.
2. Melt, then let cool to room temperature:

   2   ounces (2 squares) unsweetened chocolate.

3. Cream together in a large bowl:

   ½   cup margarine
   1   cup brown sugar.

4. Add the melted chocolate to the sugar mixture, along with:

   1   teaspoon vanilla extract.

5. Oil a 9-inch square pan.
6. Sift together:

   ⅝   cup whole wheat flour
   1   tablespoon wheat germ
   ½   teaspoon baking powder.

   Sift flour mixture once again, then add it to the liquid ingredients. Beat well.

7. Stir in:

   1   cup walnuts, chopped
   ½   cup chilled semisweet chocolate chips.

8. Spread batter in oiled pan and bake for 25 minutes, or until toothpick inserted in center comes out clean.
9. Cool completely before cutting into bars.

Butterscotch Brownies

These pack well.

1. Preheat oven to 350°F.
2. Cream together in a large bowl:

    ⅓   **cup corn oil**
    1   **cup brown sugar.**

    Beat in:

    1   **whole egg plus 1 egg white**
    1   **teaspoon vanilla extract.**
3. Mix together in a medium bowl:

    1   **cup whole wheat flour**
    1½   **teaspoons baking powder.**
4. Oil a 9-inch square pan.
5. Gradually add the flour mixture to the egg mixture, mixing just until blended. Stir in:

    1   **cup nuts, chopped**
    1   **cup unsweetened grated coconut.**
6. Spread the batter in the oiled pan and bake for 20–25 minutes, or until toothpick inserted in center comes out clean.
7. Cool completely, then cut into bars.

Honey-Oat Granola Bars

One 9" x 13" panful

1. Preheat oven to 350°F.
2. Beat together in a large bowl:

1	cup honey
1	cup corn oil
1	whole egg plus 1 egg white
1	teaspoon vanilla extract.

3. Add:

1½	cups whole wheat flour
¼	cup soya flour
¼	cup wheat germ
2	cups rolled oats
1	tablespoon ground cinnamon
2	teaspoons ground allspice
1	teaspoon ground nutmeg
1	teaspoon baking soda.

4. Stir in:

1	cup raisins
1	cup nuts, chopped
1	cup unsweetened shredded coconut.

5. Oil a 9" x 13" pan.
6. Spread the dough evenly in the pan and bake at 350°F for 20–25 minutes, or until toothpick inserted in center comes out clean.
7. Let stand for 20 minutes.
8. Heat in a small saucepan:

⅓	cup honey
3	tablespoons margarine.

9. Drizzle the honey topping evenly over the cake.
10. Let cool completely before cutting into bars.

Sierra Energy Bars

1. Preheat oven to 350°F.
2. Blend together in a large bowl:

1	cup soy oil
1	cup honey
1	whole egg plus 1 egg white
⅔	cup water
¼	cup dry milk
2	tablespoons vanilla extract
2	teaspoons ground nutmeg
2	teaspoons ground cinnamon
¼	teaspoon ground ginger.

3. Gradually add:

2	cups whole wheat flour
1	teaspoon baking soda.

4. Slowly blend in:

1	cup raisins
1	cup dates, chopped
1	cup nuts, chopped.

5. Gradually blend in:

4	cups rolled oats.

6. Oil a 12″ x 18″ rimmed baking sheet.
7. Press the dough evenly onto the oiled baking sheet.
8. Bake at 350°F for 20 minutes.
9. Cool completely before cutting into bars.

Peanut Butter Bars

1. Preheat oven to 350°F.
2. Cream together in a large bowl:

    ⅓   **cup margarine**
    ¼   **cup peanut butter**
    1   **cup honey.**

    Beat in:

    1   **whole egg plus 1 egg white**
    1   **teaspoon vanilla extract.**

3. Mix together in a medium bowl:

    1¼   **cups whole wheat flour**
    2   **tablespoons wheat germ**
    1   **teaspoon baking powder.**

4. Oil a 9" x 13" pan.

5. Gradually add the flour mixture to the honey mixture, stirring just until blended. Add:

    1   **cup unsalted peanuts, chopped**
    ¼   **cup unsweetened shredded coconut.**

6. Spread the batter in the oiled pan and bake at 350°F for 25–30 minutes, or until toothpick inserted in center comes out clean.
7. Cool completely, then cut into bars.

Scimitar Pass Energy Bars

1. Place in a large saucepan:

   ¾ cup honey
   1½ cups peanut butter.

   Stir over very low heat until smooth.

2. Remove from heat and add:

   8 cups puffed rice cereal
   1 cup unsalted, dry-roasted
   peanuts, coarsely chopped.

3. Stir well. Press firmly into an oiled 9" x 13" glass casserole dish.

4. Chill in refrigerator until firm.

5. Cut into bars.

Scottish Oat and Date Bars

1. Combine in a medium saucepan:

2	cups pitted dates, chopped
1	cup water
½	cup honey
1	tablespoon whole wheat flour.

   Simmer for 10 minutes over low heat. Add:

1	teaspoon vanilla extract.

   Set aside.

2. Preheat oven to 375°F.

3. Mix together in a medium bowl:

2	cups rolled oats
1	cup whole wheat flour
1	teaspoon baking soda.

   Gradually add and blend well:

¾	cup corn oil.

4. Oil a 9-inch square pan.

5. Spread half the oat mixture in the oiled pan. Top with the date mixture. Sprinkle the remaining oat mixture over the top. Pat down.

6. Bake at 375°F for 20 minutes, or until browned.

7. Cool completely before cutting into bars.

Lemon Bread

1. Preheat oven to 325°F.
2. Oil a 9" x 5" loaf pan.
3. Cream together in a large bowl:

    ½   **cup margarine**
    ½   **cup brown sugar.**

    Beat in:

    Finely grated rind of 2 lemons
    Juice of 2 lemons
    1   **whole egg plus 1 egg white**
    ½   **cup water**
    3   **tablespoons dry milk.**

4. Sift together in a medium bowl:

    1   **cup whole wheat flour**
    ¾   **cup unbleached white flour**
    2   **teaspoons baking powder.**

5. Gradually add the dry mixture to the liquid mixture. Beat well. Stir in:

    ½   **cup pecans, chopped.**

6. Pour the batter into the oiled pan. Bake at 325°F for 50 minutes, or until toothpick inserted in center comes out clean.

Apple Cake

1. Preheat oven to 350°F.
2. Grate and set aside:

   3 whole unpeeled tart apples.

3. Beat together in a large bowl:

   1 cup honey
   ½ cup corn oil
   1 egg.

4. Sift together in a medium bowl:

   1½ cups whole wheat flour
   2 teaspoons ground cinnamon
   1 teaspoon ground allspice
   ½ teaspoon ground nutmeg
   ½ teaspoon baking powder
   ½ teaspoon baking soda.

   Sift again.

5. Oil a 9-inch square pan.
6. Gradually add dry ingredients to liquid ones. Mix well. Stir in the grated apples, along with:

   ½ cup raisins
   ½ cup walnuts, chopped.

7. Spread the batter in the oiled pan and bake at 350°F for 50–55 minutes, or until toothpick inserted in center comes out clean.

Apple Cider Loaf

1. Preheat oven to 350°F. Oil and flour a 9" x 5" loaf pan.

2. Beat together in a large bowl:

   ½   **cup corn oil**
   ⅔   **cup honey**
   1   **whole egg plus 1 egg white.**

3. Sift together in a medium bowl:

   1¼   **cups whole wheat flour**
   ½   **cup unbleached white flour**
   1½   **teaspoons baking powder**
   1   **teaspoon ground cinnamon**
   1   **teaspoon ground allspice**
   ½   **teaspoon grated nutmeg.**

4. Add the dry ingredients to the liquid ones, alternately with:

   ½   **cup apple cider**
   1   **tablespoon lemon juice.**

   Beat well.

5. Pour the batter into the oiled pan and bake at 350°F for 30 minutes, then reduce heat to 325°F and bake for 15–20 minutes longer, or until toothpick inserted in center comes out clean.

Harvest Bread

1. Preheat oven to 350°F. Oil a 9" x 5" loaf pan.
2. Scrub but do not peel:

   1   **medium carrot**
   1   **medium zucchini.**

   Grate and set aside a total of 1¼ cups shredded carrot and zucchini.
3. Beat together in a large bowl:

   1   **whole egg plus 1 egg white**
   1   **cup honey**
   ¾   **cup soy oil.**
4. Mix together in a medium bowl:

   1   **cup whole wheat flour**
   ¼   **cup unbleached white flour**
   ¼   **cup soya flour**
   1   **teaspoon ground allspice**
   1   **teaspoon ground cinnamon**
   1   **teaspoon baking powder**
   ½   **teaspoon baking soda.**

5. Add the dry ingredients to the liquid ones, blending thoroughly. Stir in the grated carrot and zucchini, along with:

   ½   **cup raisins.**
6. Spoon the batter into the oiled pan and bake at 350°F for 30 minutes, then reduce heat to 325°F and bake for 20 minutes longer, or until toothpick inserted in center comes out clean.

Easy Cranberry Cake

1. Preheat oven to 350°F. Oil and flour an 8-inch square pan.
2. Beat together in a large bowl:

   ¾   **cup honey**
   3   **tablespoons corn oil**
   1   **egg**
   Juice of 1 lemon.
3. Mix together in a medium bowl:

   1   **cup whole wheat flour**
   1   **cup unbleached white flour**
   2   **tablespoons wheat germ**
   1   **teaspoon baking powder**
   1   **teaspoon baking soda**
   ¾   **cup pecans, chopped.**

4. Add the dry ingredients to the liquid ones, alternately with:

   1   **16-ounce can whole cranberry sauce.**

   Beat very briefly. Spread the batter in the prepared pan.
5. Bake at 350°F for 55 minutes, or until toothpick inserted in center comes out clean.

Yogurt Cake

1. Preheat oven to 325°F. Oil a 9" x 13" glass casserole dish.
2. Beat together in a large bowl:

½	cup margarine, softened
1	cup brown sugar
1	whole egg plus 1 egg white
1	cup (8 ounces) plain yogurt
1	teaspoon vanilla extract.

3. Sift together in a medium bowl:

1	cup whole wheat flour
1	cup unbleached white flour
1	teaspoon baking powder
1	teaspoon baking soda.

4. Prepare topping. Mix together in a small bowl:

½	cup brown sugar
1	tablespoon ground cinnamon
1	tablespoon whole wheat flour.

    Cut in:

3	tablespoons margarine.

    Stir in:

1	cup unsalted nuts, chopped
⅓	cup wheat germ.

    Set aside.

5. Add the flour–baking powder mixture to the yogurt mixture. Stir thoroughly. Spread the batter in the prepared baking dish.
6. Sprinkle topping evenly over the batter, and press gently.
7. Bake at 325°F for 35 minutes, or until toothpick inserted in center comes out clean.

Cinnamon Rolls

1. Beat together in a large bowl and then let stand in a warm place (unheated oven) for 15 minutes:

   1¼ **cups very warm water**
   1   **tablespoon active dry yeast**
   ½   **cup honey.**

2. Beat in:

   1   **egg**
   ½   **cup melted margarine, cooled**
   ½   **cup dry milk.**

   Add gradually:

   2½   **cups whole wheat flour**
   2   **cups unbleached white flour**
   ¼   **cup wheat germ**
   ¼   **cup soya flour.**

3. Turn out onto a floured board and knead for 10 minutes, or until smooth.

4. Replace dough in bowl. Let rise, covered, in a warm place for 50 minutes, or until double in bulk.

5. Combine and set aside:

   ½   **cup brown sugar**
   1   **tablespoon ground cinnamon**
   ¾   **cup unsalted nuts, chopped.**

6. Melt and cool:

   ½   **cup margarine.**

7. Oil a 10″ x 15″ rimmed baking sheet.

8. Punch down the dough. Divide it in half. Roll out each half into a 10″ x 16″ rectangle. Brush each rectangle with one-third of the melted margarine. Sprinkle each rectangle with half of the brown sugar mixture.

9. Roll up the rectangles, lengthwise. Seal the ends of the dough. Cut each roll into 12 pieces.

10. Stand the 24 pieces on end and place them on the baking sheet. Pour the remaining one-third of the melted margarine over the rolls.

11. Cover the rolls and let them rise in a warm place for 30 minutes. Preheat oven to 350°F.

12. Bake the rolls for 25 minutes, or until well browned. Let the rolls cool slightly.

13. Sift into a small bowl:

   1   **cup confectioners' sugar.**

14. Add:

   Juice of 1 fresh lemon.

Stir. Drizzle the icing over the rolls. Let them cool and dry completely before wrapping.

Cheddar Cheese Bread

1. Preheat oven to 350°F. Oil and flour an 8-inch square pan.
2. Beat together in a large bowl:

1	whole egg plus 1 egg white
⅓	cup olive oil
⅔	cup water
3	tablespoons brown sugar.

3. Mix together in a medium bowl:

1	cup whole wheat flour
½	cup unbleached white flour
3	tablespoons dry milk
1	teaspoon dried thyme
1	teaspoon baking powder
½	teaspoon baking soda.

4. Prepare and set aside:

1	stalk celery, minced
3	green onions, minced
8	ounces Cheddar cheese, grated
1	cup nuts, chopped.

5. Add the flour mixture to the egg mixture and beat vigorously. Stir in the nuts, cheese, and vegetables.
6. Pour batter into the prepared pan and bake at 350°F for 30 minutes, or until toothpick inserted in center comes out clean.

Savory Cheese Cakes

1. Preheat oven to 350°F.
2. Cream together:

      ½ cup margarine
      4 ounces sharp Cheddar cheese, grated
      4 ounces mozzarella cheese, grated
      2 ounces Parmesan cheese, grated
      1 teaspoon vegetable seasoning (see Salt-Free Vegetable Seasoning, Chapter Seven) or use commercial
      1 teaspoon Worcestershire sauce
      2 jalapeño chilies, fresh or canned, minced.

3. Gradually blend in:

      1⅓ cups whole wheat flour.

4. Form the dough into balls the size of small walnuts, and place them on an ungreased baking sheet. Flatten balls with the palm of your hand.
5. Bake for 12–15 minutes, or until lightly browned on bottoms.
6. When completely cool, wrap individually in plastic wrap and store in plastic bags.

Soybean "Nuts"

1. Wash:

   1   cup dried soybeans.
2. Bring to a boil:

   5   cups water.

   Add the beans and boil them for 5 minutes.
3. Turn off heat and let the beans stand overnight.
4. Drain and rinse the beans in a colander, then spread them on a towel to dry.
5. Heat in a wok or large skillet, over high heat:

   ½   inch corn oil.
6. When a heat haze forms over the oil, fry the beans one-third at a time for 6 minutes, or until very browned.
7. Drain the beans on paper towels.
8. Place in a paper bag:

   ¼   teaspoon sea salt
   ¼   teaspoon freshly ground black pepper.
9. Put the drained beans in the paper bag, close the bag tightly, and shake it vigorously.
10. Cool the "nuts" competely, then store them in zip-top plastic bags.

Nutty Snacks

Roasted Nuts

One pound

1. Preheat oven to 300°F.
2. Heat in a large cast-iron skillet:
   - 2 teaspoons olive oil.
3. Add:
   - 1 pound any unsalted shelled nuts.

   Stir until coated.
4. Add and stir until coated:
   - 1 tablespoon Worcestershire sauce
   - ½ teaspoon paprika
   - ½ teaspoon ground allspice.
5. Spread the nuts on a rimmed baking sheet and roast in 300°F oven for 15–20 minutes, stirring once.
6. Cool, then store in plastic zip-top bags.

Chili Nuts

One pound

1. Preheat oven to 300°F.
2. Heat in a large cast-iron skillet:
   - 1 tablespoon olive oil.
3. Add:
   - 1 pound any unsalted shelled nuts.

   Stir until coated.
4. Add and stir until coated:
   - 1 tablespoon chili powder
   - ½ teaspoon ground cumin
   - ½ teaspoon garlic powder.
5. Spread nuts on a rimmed baking sheet and roast in 300°F oven for 15–20 minutes, stirring once.
6. Cool, then store in plastic zip-top bags.

Curried Peanuts

One pound

1. Preheat oven to 300°F.
2. Heat in a large cast-iron skillet:

   1   **tablespoon margarine.**
3. Add:

   1   **pound unsalted peanuts**
   1   **tablespoon sunflower seed.**

   Stir until coated.
4. Add and stir until coated:

   1   **teaspoon curry powder**
   ½   **teaspoon celery seed, crushed.**
5. Spread nuts on a rimmed baking sheet and roast in a 300°F oven for 15–20 minutes, stirring once.
6. Cool, then store in plastic zip-top bags.

Tamari Nuts

One pound

1. Preheat oven to 300°F.
2. Heat in a large cast-iron skillet:

   2   **teaspoons olive oil.**
3. Add:

   1   **pound unsalted almonds, cashews, pecans, peanuts, or walnuts.**

   Stir until coated.
4. Add and stir until coated:

   1   **tablespoon tamari soy sauce**
   1   **tablespoon sesame seed**
   ½   **teaspoon garlic powder.**
5. Spread nuts on a rimmed baking sheet and roast in a 300°F oven for 15–20 minutes, stirring once.
6. Cool, then store in plastic zip-top bags.

Fruit and Vegetable Snacks

Stuffed Dates

1. Stuff pitted, dried dates with:
   Peanut butter.
2. Roll the stuffed dates in:
   Finely grated unsweetened coconut.
3. Wrap dates individually in plastic wrap, then store in a plastic bag.

Vegetable Chips

1. Slice any of the following ⅛-inch to ¼-inch thick:
   Fresh mushrooms, washed and drained
   Zucchini, or other young, tender summer squash, washed and drained
   Firm, ripe tomatoes, washed and drained
   Parsnip, scrubbed but not peeled, drained.
2. Place the slices directly on drying trays, in a single layer. Sprinkle with:
   Vegetable seasoning (see Salt-Free Vegetable Seasoning, Chapter Seven) or use commercial.
3. Dry at 145°F for 3 hours, turning once, until crisp.

Dried Fruit

Some raw fruits and vegetables need pretreatment before drying; this inhibits the action of enzymes, which can cause spoilage. The following fruits are easily dried at home, and make delicious snacks. If you use a dehydrator, the drying will take about 3 to 5 hours. If you dry the fruit in the sun, it will take a few days.

Apples

Wash, peel, and core firm, ripe apples. Slice them ¼-inch thick. Steam-blanch the slices over boiling water for 3 minutes, then plunge them into cold water and drain. Mix together 2 parts water to 1 part lemon juice; soak the slices in the solution for 3 minutes, then drain. Place slices on drying trays. Dry until firm and leathery.

Bananas

Peel ripe bananas. Cut them into ¼-inch thick slices. Soak the slices for 3 minutes in a solution of 2 parts water to 1 part lemon juice. Drain the slices, then place them on drying trays. Dry until firm and leathery.

Blueberries

Wash and drain the berries in a sieve. Bring a saucepan full of water to a boil. Dip the sieve full of berries into the boiling water for 2 minutes, then plunge into cold water. Drain the berries. Place them on drying trays and dry until berries rattle when trays are shaken.

Figs

Wash, dry, and slice tree-ripened figs in half. Place them on drying trays and dry until pliable.

Grapes

Wash and remove stems from seedless grapes. Bring a saucepan full of water to a boil. Place grapes in a sieve, then dip the grapes into the boiling water for 1 minute. Plunge them into cold water. Drain the grapes, then place them on drying trays. Dry until raisins rattle when tray is shaken.

Peaches

Wash and remove fuzz. Steam-blanch whole peaches over boiling water for 5 minutes, then plunge them into cold water and drain. Slice peaches ¼-inch to ½-inch thick. Mix together 2 parts water to 1 part lemon juice; soak the peach slices in the solution for 3 minutes, then drain. Place slices on drying trays. Dry until firm and leathery.

Pears

Wash, peel, and core ripe pears. Cut them into ¼-inch thick slices. Steam-blanch the slices over boiling water for 5 minutes, then plunge into cold water and drain. Mix together 2 parts water to 1 part lemon juice; soak the slices in the solution for 3 minutes, then drain. Place slices on drying trays. Dry until firm and leathery.

Plums

Wash and pit ripe plums. Cut them into ¼-inch thick slices. Steam-blanch the slices over boiling water for 5 minutes, then plunge into cold water and drain. Place slices on drying trays, and dry until pliable and leathery.

Trail Mix

Choose your favorite ingredients, mix them together in zip-top plastic bags, and enjoy.

Nuts

Unsalted peanuts, walnuts, pecans, pine nuts, macadamias, hickories, cashews, filberts, almonds.

Dried Fruit

Dates, raisins, currants, bananas, apples, pineapples, prunes, peaches, nectarines, apricots, figs, coarsely shredded coconut.

Seeds

Shelled sunflower or pumpkin.

Candy

Chocolate, carob, or butterscotch chips.

Miscellaneous

Popcorn, roasted soybeans (see Soybean "Nuts" in Index).

CHAPTER SIX

Car-Camping and Trailhead Cookery

Prepare these recipes in camp when you have the
luxury of fresh ingredients—butter, eggs, cheeses, fruits
and vegetables, tofu, meats, and fish. A cooler (and a
car or boat to haul it in) makes these delicious treats
possible. They're great for regular home use, too.

Wheat Griddlecakes

No eggs, salt, or fats are added.

1. Mix together:

   2½ **cups whole wheat flour**
   ½   **cup unbleached white flour**
   ¼   **cup dry milk**
   2   **tablespoons brown sugar**
   2½ **teaspoons baking powder.**

   Add:

   3½ **cups water.**

   Beat the batter thoroughly.

2. Preheat griddle slowly to medium and spread it with:

   A few drops of corn or soy oil.

   Fry the cakes until bubbling has stopped and cakes are starting to steam, then turn them and fry for a few minutes more; the cakes are done on the second side when they begin to steam. Serve hot with any of the following, if desired:

   Butter or margarine
   Yogurt
   Maple syrup.

Griddlecake Variations

Follow the recipe for Wheat Griddlecakes increasing water to 4 cups.

For Oatmeal Griddlecakes, add:

1	cup rolled oats
2	tablespoons oat bran
½	teaspoon cinnamon
½	cup raisins (optional).

For Corn Meal, add:

¾	cup corn meal.

For Buckwheat, add:

½	cup buckwheat flour.

For Coconut, add:

2	tablespoons oat or wheat bran
½	cup unsweetened shredded coconut
½	cup nuts, chopped.

For Apple, add:

2	washed, cored, and grated but not peeled apples
¼	cup wheat germ
½	teaspoon cinnamon.

For Peach or Apricot, add:

2	washed, pitted, and sliced but not peeled peaches or apricots
¼	cup wheat germ
¼	teaspoon cinnamon.

For Banana, add:

¼	cup wheat germ, or oat or wheat bran
2	thinly sliced ripe bananas.

For Berry, add:

¼	cup wheat germ
½	cup berries.

Three Egg Omelette

1. Prepare filling if desired, and set aside.
   For mushroom filling, sauté:

   > 6   **fresh mushrooms, sliced, in 1 teaspoon olive oil, until soft.**

   For herb filling, combine:

   > 4   **sprigs parsley, minced**
   > 3   **green onions, minced**
   > 2   **teaspoons any fresh herbs, minced, or 1 teaspoon dried.**

   For cheese filling, grate:

   > ¾   **cup any cheese.**

2. Break into a bowl:

   > 3   **eggs.**

   Add:

   > 1   **tablespoon water**
   > ¼   **teaspoon freshly ground black pepper**
   > ⅛   **teaspoon sea salt.**

   Beat the eggs very lightly until just blended.

3. Heat an omelette pan, slowly, until it is very hot. Add to the pan:

   > 1   **tablespoon olive oil.**

   When the oil is hot, quickly pour in the egg mixture. Keep the pan moving with one hand, while you stir the eggs with the other. Keep lifting the cooked portion of the egg to allow the uncooked portion to run into the bottom of the pan. When the eggs are half cooked, quickly place the filling on top of them.

4. Fold the omelette in half, and cover the pan. Move the pan to the edge of the fire and allow the omelette to cook over very low heat for 1 minute. Serve immediately.

Matzoh Egg

A light meal, good any time.

1. Beat together lightly in a bowl:

   2   **whole eggs plus 6 egg whites**
   2   **tablespoons water**
   ½   **teaspoon sea salt**
   ½   **teaspoon freshly ground black pepper.**

   Add:

   6   **matzoh crackers, crumbled into bite-sized pieces.**

   Let the mixture stand for 10 minutes.

2. Heat a large cast-iron skillet over high heat, then add:

   2   **tablespoons corn or soy oil.**

   When the oil is hot, add:

   1   **onion, finely chopped.**

   Sauté for about 5 minutes, until onion is browned, then reduce heat to low.

3. Add the egg mixture to the skillet. Stir and cook gently until the eggs are set.

Healthy Sandwiches

Salad Sandwiches

Eight sandwiches

1. Mix together in a bowl:

   2   large tomatoes, chopped
   10 pitted ripe olives, minced
   4   green onions, minced
   2   tablespoons light olive oil
   2   teaspoons red wine vinegar
   ½   teaspoon freshly ground black pepper
   ¼   teaspoon sea salt.

2. Split:

   4   large crusty sandwich rolls.

   Spread the tomato mixture on the rolls.

3. Slice thinly:

   ½   **pound mild cheese.**

   Lay the cheese slices on top of the filling. Serve with:

   Lettuce (optional).

Tofu "Egg" Salad

Serves 4

1. Rinse and drain:

   1   **pound raw firm tofu.**

   Wrap the tofu in a towel and gently press out as much moisture as possible.

2. Put the tofu in a bowl with:

   1   teaspoon ground turmeric
   5   green onions, minced
   3   tablespoons mayonnaise
   2   ribs celery, minced
   Few grains sea salt
   Dash of cayenne pepper.

3. Mix well, mashing the tofu into fairly small pieces. Serve on any bread or crackers.

Grilled Carrot Sandwiches

Sixteen sandwiches

1. Heat grill over medium fire or flame.
2. Mix together in a large bowl:

   8   small tender carrots, scrubbed but not peeled, grated
   4   green onions, minced
   2   tablespoons Dijon mustard
   5   tablespoons plain yogurt or mayonnaise
   ½   teaspoon vegetable seasoning (see Salt-Free Vegetable Seasoning, Chapter Seven) or use commercial
   Few grains sea salt.

3. Grill until light brown on one side:

   16   slices of bread.

4. Turn the bread, spread with carrot mixture, and place on top of sandwiches:

   16   thinly sliced pieces of cheese.

5. Grill until cheese is melted and filling is very hot.

Cream Cheese Sandwich Spread

Eight sandwiches

1. Bring to room temperature:

   16   ounces cream cheese.

2. Mix cream cheese with:

   ⅓   cup minced fresh herbs (thyme, parsley, cilantro, chives, marjoram, singly or in combination)
   ¼   cup milk.

3. Spread on:

   8   slices of bread.

Omelette Sandwiches

Four sandwiches

1. Heat a cast-iron skillet over high heat, then add:

   2   **tablespoons olive oil.**

   Add:

   2   **onions, chopped.**

   When onions start to brown, reduce heat to low and add:

   2   **bell peppers, chopped**
   4   **whole tomatoes, chopped**
   2   **cloves garlic, minced**
   2   **tablespoons dried Italian seasoning**
   ½   **teaspoon sea salt.**

   Simmer for 20 minutes.

2. Beat lightly in a bowl:

   2   **whole eggs plus 6 egg whites**
   2   **tablespoons water**

   2   **tablespoons vegetable seasoning (see Salt-Free Vegetable Seasoning, Chapter Seven) or use commercial.**

3. In a separate omelette pan, heat over high flame:

   1   **tablespoon olive oil.**

   When the oil is hot, add the eggs. Keep the pan moving, and gently lift the eggs to allow the runny parts to cook. Fold the omelette in half, reduce heat to very low, cover, and cook for 3 minutes.

4. Pour the cooked vegetables onto:

   4   **split lightly toasted sandwich rolls.**

   Sprinkle with:

   10   **sprigs parsley, minced.**

5. Divide omelette in four, and place the divided pieces in the sandwiches, on top of the vegetables.

Potato Salad Vinaigrette

1. Cut into 1″ x 1½″ chunks and boil gently for 20 minutes, or until just tender:

    15 small new potatoes, scrubbed but not peeled.

2. While the potatoes are cooking, blend in a large bowl:

    1   cup red wine or cider vinegar
    ¼   cup light olive oil
    1   teaspoon sea salt
    1   teaspoon vegetable seasoning (see Salt-Free Vegetable Seasoning, Chapter Seven) or use commercial
    ½   teaspoon dry mustard
    1   teaspoon fresh minced thyme, or ½ teaspoon dried
    1   clove garlic, minced.

3. As soon as the potatoes are just tender, drain them quickly in a colander and immediately marinate them in the vinaigrette dressing.

4. Allow the salad to cool to room temperature.

5. Add to the salad:

    3   ribs celery, chopped
    3   small carrots, scrubbed but not peeled, grated
    1   sweet onion, finely minced
    4   hard-boiled eggs, chopped
    10 sprigs fresh parsley or cilantro, finely minced.

6. The salad may be eaten at room temperature or chilled. Serve with:

    Lettuce or spinach leaves (optional).

Vegetable Sushi

1. Mix together in a large bowl:

    1¼ **cups vinegar (rice vinegar or cider vinegar)**

    3 **tablespoons honey or sugar**

    1½ **teaspoons sea salt.**

2. Cook:

    4 **servings Brown Rice (see Chapter Seven).**

    Cook the rice thoroughly until it is very dry and fluffy.

3. While the rice is hot, add it to the vinegar mixture. Stir thoroughly, then let it stand.

4. Cook:

    4 **servings Stir-Fried Vegetables (see Chapter Seven).**

    Sauté the vegetables until very browned, then add soy sauce, cover, and let cook until well done, about 10 minutes.

5. Add the cooked vegetables to the marinated rice, along with:

    10 **green onions, minced**
    20 **sprigs fresh parsley, minced.**

Mix together thoroughly.

6. Toast over an open flame:

    5 **sheets nori sea vegetable, 7" x 8" size.**

    The nori is toasted when its color changes from black to greenish brown.

7. Lay the toasted nori on a board. Divide the rice into 5 portions, and lay the rice on one edge of each nori sheet.

8. Dampen your hands with cold water, and squeeze the rice into round shapes which cover the full length of the nori. Roll up the rice-filled nori sheets. Seal the edges with a little cold water.

9. Place the nori rolls on a plate. Seal them in a plastic bag and chill for several hours, or overnight.

10. Cut the nori rolls crosswise, 10 pieces per roll, for a total of 50 pieces.

11. Stand rolls on end and arrange them on a serving platter. Cover the top of each roll with:

    Prepared horseradish (optional).

Tabbouleh (Bulgur Wheat Salad)

1. Cook:

>   4   servings Bulgur Wheat (see Chapter Seven).

2. Place the bulgur in a sieve, rinse it with cold water, and let it drain. Put the bulgur in a cloth towel and squeeze out as much moisture as possible.

3. Mix together in a large bowl:

>   **Juice of 4 fresh lemons (about 1 cup of juice)**
>   ⅔   **cup light olive oil**
>   3   **whole fresh tomatoes, chopped**
>   2   **cups parsley leaves, chopped**
>   1   **cup mint leaves, chopped**
>   2   **cloves garlic, minced**
>   5   **green onions, minced**
>   3   **teaspoons sea salt**
>   1   **teaspoon freshly ground black pepper**
>   **Dash of cayenne pepper.**

4. Marinate the bulgur in the dressing for 30 minutes, then serve the salad with:

>   **Lettuce or spinach leaves.**

Rice and Tuna Salad

1. Cook:

   4   servings Brown Rice (see Chapter Seven).

2. Mix together in a large bowl:

   1   cup cider or red wine vinegar
   ⅓   cup olive oil
   1   teaspoon honey
   1   teaspoon vegetable seasoning (see Salt-Free Vegetable Seasoning, Chapter Seven) or use commercial
   1   teaspoon sea salt
   1   teaspoon minced fresh thyme, or 2 teaspoons dried
   1   clove garlic, minced
   Dash of cayenne pepper.

3. Marinate the hot, cooked brown rice in the dressing and allow it to cool slightly.

4. Add to the rice:

   5   ribs celery, chopped
   1   bell pepper, chopped
   1   sweet onion, minced
   10   sprigs parsley, minced
   10   sprigs cilantro, minced (optional)
   1   12½-ounce can water-packed Albacore tuna, drained and flaked.

5. Serve immediately on a bed of:

   Lettuce or spinach leaves (optional).

Marinated Tofu Salad

1. Rinse and drain:

   1   pound firm tofu.

2. Mix together in a large bowl:

   ½   cup red wine vinegar
   ¼   cup light olive oil
   2½   tablespoons tamari soy sauce
   2   cloves garlic, minced
   Hot sauce to taste.

3. Slice or crumble the tofu into the above dressing.
   Stir in:

   2   carrots, grated
   2   stalks celery, chopped
   2   cups bean sprouts
   ¾   cup unsalted nuts, chopped.

4. Chill briefly in ice chest or refrigerator. Serve with:

   Lettuce or spinach leaves.

5. May be used as a sandwich spread.

Macadamia Chicken Salad

Eight cups

1. Remove skin from:

    4   chicken breasts.

    Place them on:

    4   large pieces of aluminum foil, dull side out.

    Sprinkle with:

    ⅓   cup dry white wine
    Freshly ground black pepper.

    Seal the foil tightly. Cook the chicken over a hot campfire for 15 minutes, then turn the chicken and cook 15 minutes longer. Cool the meat, then dice it.

2. Mix together in a large bowl:

    ⅔   cup olive oil
    ½   cup red wine vinegar
    1   teaspoon vegetable seasoning (see Salt-Free Vegetable Seasoning, Chapter Seven) or use commercial
    1   teaspoon fresh thyme, minced, or ½ teaspoon dried

    1   teaspoon paprika
    Sea salt to taste.

3. Add the diced chicken, along with:

    2   carrots, grated
    1   onion, grated
    4   ribs celery, finely chopped
    1   cup macadamia nuts, coarsely chopped
    Mayonnaise to taste.

4. Serve the salad immediately, or chill it.

5. Serve with:

    Lettuce or spinach leaves (optional).

Chef's Special Salad

A complete meal in itself.

1. Mix together in a 2½-quart bowl:

¾	cup any vinegar
½	cup olive oil
1	teaspoon dried mustard
1	teaspoon any fresh herb, minced, or ½ teaspoon dried
1	teaspoon sea salt.

2. Add any of the following:

1	15-ounce can any beans, drained and rinsed
	Cucumbers, thinly sliced
	Bean sprouts
	Carrots, scrubbed but not peeled, grated
	Celery, chopped.

   Also add any of the following vegetables, cooked until just tender, then drained:

   Green beans
   Peas
   Potatoes
   Cauliflower
   Beets.

3. Place the salad in an ice chest or refrigerator, and marinate for 1 hour or longer.

4. Add to the salad any of the following:

   Any nutmeats
   Sunflower seeds, shelled
   Chives, minced
   Green onions, minced
   Parsley, minced
   Tomatoes, cut into chunks
   Bell peppers, sliced
   Pitted olives
   Seedless grapes
   Raisins
   Hard-boiled eggs, sliced
   Cooked shrimp
   Any cheese, grated
   Cabbage, finely chopped
   Spinach, torn by hand
   Any lettuce, torn by hand.

5. Toss well, then serve.

Ultimate Lentil Burgers

1. Wash:

   1½ cups lentils.

   Cover with:

   4½ cups cold water.

   Boil, then reduce heat and simmer for 30 minutes; do not overcook. Pour into a colander and drain for 30 minutes.

2. Place lentils in a cloth towel, squeeze out as much moisture as possible, and put them in a large bowl with:

½	**cup raw wheat germ**
1	**teaspoon sea salt**
2	**tablespoons chili powder**
½	**teaspoon freshly ground black pepper**
1	**small bell pepper, minced**
2	**scallions, minced**
2	**cloves garlic, minced.**

3. Mix well and form into patties. Dust with:

   Whole wheat flour.

   Heat in a large heavy skillet:

   4 tablespoons olive oil.

   Fry burgers over medium high heat until dark brown, then turn the burgers and place on top:

   4 pieces thinly sliced cheese.

   Cook until the cheese is melted.

4. Serve with:

4	**hamburger buns**
	Lettuce
	Catsup.

Anywhere Burgers

Four burgers

1. Mix together:

> 2   **cups TVP (Textured Vegetable Protein)**
> 1   **cup raw wheat germ**
> ¼   **teaspoon curry powder**
> **Dash cayenne pepper**
> 1   **teaspoon sea salt.**

2. Add:

> 2   **cups boiling water.**

Mix well and allow to stand, covered, for 1 hour.

3. Form into patties. Dust with:

> **Whole wheat flour.**

Heat in a large heavy skillet:

> 3   **tablespoons olive oil.**

Fry burgers over high heat until dark brown, then turn the burgers and place on top:

> 4   **pieces thinly sliced cheese.**

Cook until the cheese is melted.

4. Place on:

> 4   **hamburger buns.**

5. Serve with the following sauce, if desired:

> 2   **tablespoons mayonnaise or yogurt**
> 2   **tablespoons catsup**
> 2   **green onions, minced**
> 1   **jalapeño chilie, minced.**

Spaghetti with TVP "Meatballs"

Serve with a green salad.

1. Prepare:

   Anywhere Burgers, (see preceding recipe).

   Divide into 16 portions and roll into balls, turning frequently to brown all sides.

2. Add to the skillet of fried TVP balls:

   2 cups commercial tomato sauce.

   Heat the sauce gently.

3. Cook:

   12 ounces dried spaghetti.

   Drain it in a colander.

4. Divide the spaghetti onto four plates or into four bowls. Place four lentil balls on each serving, then pour the tomato sauce over all.

Quesadillas

Mexican grilled cheese sandwiches.

1. Grate and set aside:

   3-4 cups grated cheese.

2. Chop and set aside:

   6 jalapeño chilies, fresh or canned, finely chopped

   6 green onions, chopped, or 1 sweet onion, minced.

3. Prepare:

   12 Flour Tortillas or 16 Corn Tortillas (see Chapter Seven).

   Keep the tortillas warm in a folded towel placed inside a tightly closed plastic bag.

4. Sprinkle the grated cheese, chilies, and onion on the tortillas. Reheat them, a few at a time, over medium heat on a griddle, just until the cheese melts.

5. Fold the quesadillas in half and eat them out of hand.

Soft Tacos

1. For **Bean Tacos**, prepare:

    4   **servings Chili Beans (see Index) or use 4 cups canned refried beans.**

    For **Vegetable Tacos**, prepare:

    4   **servings Stir-Fried Vegetables (see Chapter Seven).**

2. Grate and set aside:

    1   **cup any cheese.**

3. Finely chop and set aside:

    2   **cups lettuce, spinach, or cabbage.**

4. Prepare:

    12   **Flour Tortillas (see Chapter Seven) or use commercial tortillas.**

As each tortilla is cooked, place in folded cloth towel inside of a large plastic bag. Keep bag tightly closed.

5. To assemble tacos, fill with cooked beans or vegetables; grated cheese; lettuce, spinach, or cabbage; and:

    Hot sauce to taste.

Fold each taco up from the bottom, then roll from one side to the other. Eat out of hand.

Tempura

1. Cook:

    4   servings Brown Rice (see
         Chapter Seven).

2. Prepare tempura sauce. Stir together in a saucepan
   and heat gently:

    ½   cup bean liquid, stock, or water
    ¼   cup soy sauce
    2   tablespoons sweet rice wine, or
         sherry
    1   tablespoon honey or sugar
         Dash of powdered ginger.

3. Scrub and slice any of the following vegetables,
   shrimp, or meat for a total of 3 cups:

    Mushrooms, halved
    Onion, sliced and separated into
        rings
    Zucchini, thinly sliced
    Green beans, ends trimmed
    Bell pepper, cut into squares
    Carrots, thinly sliced
    Potato, unpeeled, thinly sliced
    Sweet potato, unpeeled, thinly sliced
    Eggplant, thinly sliced
    Green onions, trimmed

Nori sea vegetable, cut into squares
    (dip only one side of nori into
    batter)
Whole peeled shrimps, tails left on
1½-inch chunks any lean meat.

4. Prepare tempura batter. Mix together in a bowl:

    2   cups whole wheat flour
    1   teaspoon sea salt
    1   teaspoon baking powder.

   Add and mix gently; do not beat:

    2¼   cups very cold water.

5. Heat a wok or cast-iron Dutch oven over high
   heat. Add to the pot:

    2½   inches of corn or soy oil.

6. When the oil is very hot, dip the prepared
   vegetables, shrimp, or meat, a few pieces at a time,
   into the tempura batter, and slide them into the
   hot oil. Cook until browned, turning them once.
   Drain the pieces on clean paper bags and keep
   them warm near the fire.

7. Pour tempura sauce into four separate bowls. Dip
   tempura pieces into sauce and eat along with the
   brown rice.

Miso Soup

Quick, delicious soup.

1. Soak in 9 cups of cold water:

    **1   sheet of nori sea vegetable,
7" x 8", cut into 1-inch squares.**

2. Heat a cast-iron Dutch oven over high heat. Add:

    1   tablespoon soy oil.

When the oil is hot, add:

    **1   large onion, thinly sliced
longitudinally.**

Stir-fry the onion for 1 minute, then add:

    1   carrot, thinly sliced diagonally.

Sauté for 5 minutes, stirring occasionally, then add:

    4   cabbage leaves, shredded.

Sauté for 5 minutes, then add the nori and water. Bring to a boil, then simmer until vegetables are tender.

3. Mix together:

    **3   tablespoons miso (fermented
soybean paste)**

    **2   tablespoons tahini (sesame seed
butter)**

    ½   cup water.

Add to the soup. Cook the soup for 10 minutes longer.

Campfire Baked Potatoes

1. Scrub:

   4   large Idaho baking potatoes.

2. Make a 3-inch long slit in each potato, and insert in the slits a mixture of:

   6   tablespoons butter or margarine
   1   clove garlic, minced
   Freshly ground black pepper to taste
   Sea salt to taste.

3. Wrap the potatoes individually in aluminum foil, dull side of foil out.

4. Place the potatoes in the hot campfire coals and bake for 1 hour.

Griddle Biscuits

1. Preheat a cast-iron griddle over medium-low flame.
2. Mix together:

    1¼ cups whole wheat flour
    ½   cup unbleached white flour
    1   tablespoon wheat germ
    2½ teaspoons baking powder
    Few grains of sea salt.

3. Cut in:

    3   tablespoons unsalted butter or
        margarine.

   Add:

    ⅔   cup milk.

4. Stir very briefly and turn onto a lightly floured board. Knead for a few seconds, then roll out ¼-inch to ½-inch thick. Cut dough into 12 pieces. Separate biscuits.
5. Lightly sprinkle griddle with:

    ½   teaspoon corn meal.

   Bake the biscuits for 5 minutes on one side, then turn and cook 5 minutes more.

Cooking griddle biscuits over a campfire.

Skillet Corn Bread

1. Heat a cast-iron skillet over a medium flame.
2. Mix together in a large bowl or pot:

   1 **cup polenta (coarse-grained corn meal)**
   ¾ **cup whole wheat flour**
   ¼ **cup unbleached white flour**
   3 **tablespoons instant dry milk**
   2½ **teaspoons baking powder**
   1 **tablespoon brown sugar**
   Few grains of sea salt.

3. Beat together in a separate bowl:

   ⅞ **cup water**
   1 **egg**
   2 **tablespoons corn or soy oil.**

4. Add to skillet and heat:

   1 **teaspoon oil.**

5. Combine liquid ingredients with dry ones and stir until just blended. Pour into skillet and bake, covered, for about 30 minutes, or until toothpick inserted in center comes out clean. Check periodically and reduce heat if necessary.

Griddle Oatcakes

These cracker-like cakes are excellent either cooked over a campfire, or prepared at home and carried in your knapsack.

1. Mix together:

1½	**cups oat flour (rolled oats ground fine in a blender)**
½	**teaspoon sea salt**
¼	**teaspoon baking soda.**

2. Cut in:

2	**tablespoons margarine.**

3. Add:

8	**tablespoons hot water.**

4. Preheat griddle to medium heat.
5. Mix the oatcakes, then turn them out onto a board which has been liberally sprinkled with more oat flour.
6. Divide dough into 8 pieces and roll out each piece as thinly as possible.
7. Cook the cakes on the ungreased griddle, turning them frequently, until light brown.

Vanilla or Chocolate Pudding

No eggs or fresh milk are needed to make this instant dessert.

1. Mix together in a bowl:

4	**cups water**
1	**cup instant dry milk.**

2. Mix together in a cast-iron Dutch oven:

½	**cup honey, white sugar, or brown sugar**
6	**tablespoons cornstarch**
¼	**teaspoon sea salt.**

3. For chocolate pudding, add:

4	**tablespoons unsweetened cocoa powder.**

4. Very gradually, add the milk to the ingredients in the Dutch oven.

5. Cook the pudding over low heat, stirring constantly. When it boils, allow it to simmer for 2 minutes, while stirring vigorously.

6. Remove the pudding from the heat and stir in:

2	**tablespoons butter or margarine**
1	**teaspoon vanilla extract.**

7. Serve warm, or chilled. May be served plain or with:

   Shredded coconut
   Chopped nutmeats
   Any fresh fruit.

Indian Pudding

Old-fashioned hasty pudding.

1. Mix together in the top half of a double boiler and bring to a boil over direct heat:

4	cups water
1	cup dry milk.

2. Add very gradually, stirring constantly:

½	cup corn meal.

3. Place the top half of double boiler over the bottom half and steam the pudding for 10 minutes. Then add:

¾	cup raisins
½	cup honey
¼	cup dark molasses
4	tablespoons butter or margarine
½	teaspoon cinnamon
¼	teaspoon sea salt
¼	teaspoon powdered ginger.

4. Steam the pudding, stirring occasionally, for 20 minutes.

5. Serve the pudding warm with:

   Milk or yogurt (optional).

Fruit Desserts

Fresh Fruit

Serves 4

1. Wash and slice into four bowls:

   5   cups mixture of any ripe fruits.

2. Sprinkle with any of the following:

   **Shredded coconut
   Chopped nuts
   Raisins
   Shelled sunflower seed.**

3. Serve with:

   Yogurt (optional).

Campfire Baked Apples

Serves 4

1. Wash and core:

   4   large cooking apples.

   Fill the cores with a mixture of:

   **4   tablespoons butter or margarine
   4   tablespoons honey or brown
        sugar
   1   teaspoon cinnamon
   ½   teaspoon allspice.**

2. Wrap the apples individually in aluminum foil, dull side of foil out.

3. Place apples in the hot campfire coals and bake for 45 minutes.

CHAPTER SEVEN

Basic Recipes

Steaming grain in a double boiler.

Grains

Brown Rice

Serves 4

1. Wash thoroughly and drain:

   1¾ cups raw brown rice.

   Place the rice in the top half of a double boiler with:

   2¼ cups cold water
   ¼ teaspoon sea salt
   1 whole bay leaf (optional).

   Bring to a boil, then simmer for 50 minutes, or until water level falls below level of rice. Remove bay leaf. Stir the rice.

2. Place 1 inch of water in the bottom half of double boiler, and bring to a boil. Place top half of double boiler over bottom. Reduce heat to low, then steam the rice for 20 minutes. Turn off the heat and allow rice to stand for 5 minutes before serving.

Bulgur Wheat

Serves 4

1. Place in the top half of a double boiler:

   3½ cups bulgur
   4½ cups cold water.

   Bring to a boil.

2. Place 1 inch of water in the bottom half of double boiler, and bring to a boil. Place top half of double boiler over bottom. Reduce heat, then steam the bulgur until it is fluffy, about 20 minutes.

3. Stir in:

   ½ teaspoon sea salt.

   Fluff with a fork and serve.

Couscous

1. Bring to a boil:

       2⅓ **cups water**
       1   **tablespoon margarine**
       Few grains sea salt.

2. Add to boiling water:

       2   **cups couscous.**

   Stir, then turn off heat. Cover tightly and let stand 6 minutes. Fluff with fork when done.

Kasha (Buckwheat Groats)

1. Brown in a cast-iron skillet over medium heat:

       1½ **cups raw (unroasted) kasha.**

   When the kasha begins to brown, turn off the heat and continue to stir.

2. Bring to a boil in the top half of a double boiler:

       3   **cups water**
       ½   **teaspoon sea salt**
       ½   **teaspoon freshly ground black pepper.**

3. Add the toasted kasha to the water, and bring to a boil. Put 1 inch of water in the bottom half of the double boiler and bring to a boil. Place top of double boiler over bottom. Reduce heat and steam the kasha for 20 minutes, or until tender.

Millet

1. Wash, and drain in a sieve:

    1½ cups raw millet.

2. Bring to a boil in the top half of a double boiler:

    3½ cups water

    1   teaspoon vegetable seasoning (see Salt-Free Vegetable Seasoning in this chapter or use commercial)

    1   teaspoon sea salt.

    Add the millet to the boiling water.

3. Put 1 inch of water in the bottom half of the double boiler and bring to a boil. Place top of double boiler over bottom. Reduce heat and steam the millet for 25 minutes, or until tender.

Polenta (Coarse-Grained Corn Meal)

Serves 4

1. Place in the top half of a double boiler and bring to a boil, stirring frequently:

    3   cups milk

    1   tablespoon margarine

    ½   teaspoon vegetable seasoning (see Salt-Free Vegetable Seasoning in this chapter or use commercial)

    ½   teaspoon sea salt.

2. Add slowly, stirring constantly:

    ¾   cup polenta.

Cook over direct heat for a few minutes. Place 1 inch of water in the bottom half of a double boiler, and bring to a boil. Place top half of double boiler over bottom. Reduce heat to very low, then steam the polenta for 10 minutes, or until it is very thick and smooth.

Dried Beans and Lentils

To Cook Dried Beans

*One cup dried beans
yields two to three cups
cooked beans*

1. Measure beans.
2. Wash and sort beans. Drain in a colander.
3. Boil water in a large pot; use at least 3 times as much water as volume of dried beans.
4. When water is at a full boil, add the beans and boil them for 2 minutes.
5. Turn off heat and let beans stand, covered, for 2 hours.
6. Drain beans into a colander and rinse them thoroughly.
7. Replace beans in pot and cover with fresh water.
8. Bring to a boil, then simmer until beans are soft.

Lentils

Serves 4

1. Wash, pick over and drain:

   1   cup lentils.

   Put the lentils in a saucepan with:

   2¼ cups cold water.

2. Bring to a boil, then simmer for 35 minutes, or until just tender.
3. Season with:

   ½   teaspoon sea salt
   ½   teaspoon freshly ground black pepper.

Stir-Fried Vegetables

1. Scrub, then chop or slice any of the vegetables listed in Step 3, keeping each variety separate. You need a total of:

   4   cups cleaned chopped vegetables.

2. Heat in a cast-iron Dutch oven or wok over high heat:

   2   tablespoons oil (olive, soy, corn, or safflower).

3. When a haze just begins to form above the oil, add any of the following vegetables, one variety at a time, in the order listed. Cook and stir each vegetable addition for a few minutes before adding the next:

   Onion, chopped or sliced
   Carrots, chopped or thinly sliced
   Broccoli stalk, chopped
   Zucchini, thinly sliced
   Eggplant, chopped
   Broccoli flowerettes, separated
   Mushrooms, quartered
   Green beans, sliced
   Bell peppers, sliced
   Cabbage leaves, chopped
   Peas
   Celery ribs, thinly sliced.

4. Turn heat to low and add, stirring well:

   Soy sauce to taste
   Chopped green onions
   Chopped parsley.

5. Cover and cook very briefly, until vegetables are barely tender.

6. If desired, serve with cooked grain, chapaties, or tortillas (see Index).

Thick Tomato Sauce

Six cups of sauce

This simple sauce will keep at least one week in refrigerator, 18 months in freezer. It improves with age.

1. Heat in cast-iron skillet over high flame:

   1   tablespoon olive oil.

   Add and sauté until transparent:

   2   onions, minced.

   Reduce heat to very low, and cook slowly until very brown.

2. Place in blender, a small portion at a time:

   10   pounds very ripe tomatoes (about 30 tomatoes), washed and cored but not peeled
   3   bell peppers, washed and cored
   3   cloves garlic, halved and peeled
   2   chile peppers, washed and seeded
   ½   cup fresh oregano, or 4 tablespoons dried.

   The juice from the ripe tomatoes will serve as liquid to grind the other vegetables, so include some tomatoes in each portion of vegetables

Grinding vegetables in a blender.

ground. As you grind each portion of vegetables, put them in a large stock pot. When all the vegetables have been ground, bring them to a boil.

3. Add the sautéed onions to the tomato mixture, along with:

   1   6-ounce can tomato paste.

   Reduce the heat to very low and simmer, partially covered, until thick, about 5 hours.

196

Fresh Pasta

A pasta machine speeds the kneading, rolling, and cutting, but it is not essential. Pasta can be easily rolled and cut by hand.

1. Mix together on board or countertop:

1	**cup whole wheat flour**
1	**cup unbleached white flour.**

2. Mix together lightly in a small bowl:

2	**eggs**
3	**tablespoons olive oil**
3	**tablespoons water**
½	**teaspoon sea salt.**

Cutting pasta.

3. Make a well in the flour, and pour in the egg mixture. Knead well, then seal dough in a plastic bag and let it stand for 1 hour.

4. Divide the dough into 8 pieces, and roll out each piece as thinly as possible. Dry the pasta for about 30 minutes by draping the sheets of dough over wire coat hangers which have been covered with waxed paper.

5. Roll up the sheets of pasta and cut them into noodles with a sharp knife.
   Separate the individual strands.

6. In a large saucepan, boil 2½ quarts of water. Drop the pasta into the boiling water and cook it very briefly, about 3 minutes. Drain the pasta in a colander. Serve immediately.

Drying pasta.

197

Gloria's Flour Tortillas

1. Mix together:

3	cups La Piña tortilla flour
1	cup whole wheat flour
½	teaspoon sea salt
2	teaspoons baking powder.

2. Cut in, using your hands:

¼	cup manteca (lard), or solid vegetable shortening.

3. Add:

1½	cups very hot water.

4. Mix and knead briefly until smooth. Cover and let stand at room temperature for 2 hours. Chill in refrigerator or ice chest for 6 hours, or overnight.

5. Bring dough out of cooler or refrigerator for 1 hour and allow to warm slightly.

6. Preheat griddle to medium. Divide dough into 12 pieces and roll out on lightly floured board, making the tortillas as thin as possible.

Rolling tortillas.

7. Cook tortillas on ungreased griddle, turning them frequently, until very light brown. As each tortilla is done, place in folded cloth towel inside of a large plastic bag. Keep bag tightly closed. Serve as soon as all tortillas are cooked.

8. To store tortillas for backpack trips, allow them to cool completely. Wrap in aluminum foil, then double-bag in plastic. Reheat tortillas in foil over fire or stove.

Corn Tortillas

1. Mix together:

2	**cups masa harina de maiz (corn tortilla flour)**
½	**teaspoon sea salt**
2	**cups boiling water.**

2. Cover dough and let stand for 30 minutes to 1 hour.

3. Heat a cast-iron griddle over medium heat.

4. Divide dough into 16 balls and roll out each ball between 2 pieces of waxed paper, or press in a tortilla press which has been lined with waxed paper.

5. Cook tortillas one at a time, turning them frequently, until they are light brown.

6. As each tortilla is done, place it in a folded cloth towel inside of a plastic bag. Keep the bag tightly closed. Serve as soon as all the tortillas are cooked.

Salt-Free Vegetable Seasoning

1. Spread directly on drying trays:

> 3   **cups fresh rosemary leaves**
> 3   **cups fresh basil leaves**
> 3   **cups fresh mint leaves**
> 2   **cups fresh parsley sprigs**
> 4   **medium carrots, grated**
> **Rind of 2 fresh lemons, finely grated**
> 3   **bell peppers, finely chopped**
> 1   **jalapeño chile, finely chopped**
> 2   **large onions, thinly sliced and separated**
> 4   **cloves garlic, thinly sliced**
> ¾   **cup sesame seed**
> ¼   **cup celery seed.**

2. Dehydrate for 5 hours at 145°F.

3. Pour the dried vegetables into a dry blender. Grind to a coarse powder.

4. Store in opaque glass or ceramic jars.

5. Keep some handy in a shaker for table and cooking use.

Bibliography

Beard, James A. **Beard on Bread**. New York: Alfred A. Knopf, 1973.

Braue, John R. **Uncle John's Original Bread Book**. Florida: Exposition Press, 1965.

DeLong, Deanna. **How to Dry Foods**. Tucson, Arizona: H.P. Books, 1979.

Ewald, Ellen Buchman. **Recipes for a Small Planet**. New York: Ballantine Books, 1975.

Fletcher, Colin. **The Complete Walker III**. New York: Alfred A. Knopf, 1984.

Lappe, Frances Moore. **Diet for a Small Planet**. New York: Ballantine Books, 1975.

MacManiman, Gen. **Dry It—You'll Like It!** Fall City, Washington: Living Foods Dehydrators, 1974.

Rombauer, Irma S. and Marion R. Becker. **Joy of Cooking**. New York: Bobbs-Merrill, 1975.

Index

Please send me your camp cookery questions and suggestions.

Thank you,
Linda F. Yaffe
P.O. Box 4820
Auburn, California 95604